Educational Planning

EDUCATIONAL PLANNING

Dr. R.K. Raghuram

CRESCENT
PUBLISHING CORPORATION

[The responsibility for the facts stated, conclusions reached and plagiarism, if any, in this book is entirely that of the Author. And the Publisher bears no responsibility for them, whatsoever.]

Educational Planning

Published : 2018

ISBN 978-81-8342-145-4

Published by :

CRESCENT PUBLISHING CORPORATION
4831/24, Prahlad Street,
Ansari Road, Darya Ganj,
New Delhi - 110002
Ph. : 23272541, 23257835
Fax : 91- 011- 23257835
e-mail : campusbooks@hotmail.com

Printed at :
Roshan Offset Printers
Delhi

Preface

Education has always been a matter of immense priority for governments and nations. Throughout history, societies have sought to educate their people to produce goods and services, respond creatively to their environment and satiate their aesthetic impulses. Today, as education becomes a key indicator for development, the attention and thrust on it has become far more conspicuous and pressing . In developing countries like India, where a major part of the population is still illiterate, education has also become a rallying point for politicians even as they recognise the allure of an educated life for the downtrodden masses.

Here setting-up of schools and colleges, however, is not the key to propagate education. As the need for education becomes ever more pressing, commercialisation becoming a priority, and quality and standards being acknowledged as imperative, educational planning is no longer an issue which can be sidelined. This book in the encylopaedia of development and planning of education concentrates its focus on this issue of planning in education.

The book is a comprehensive manual which analyses educational planning in all its aspects. Educational planning is an endeavour which needs incorporate only the best managerial skills and administrators, and as such, is a Herculean task with its myriad responsibilities. The book is a guide on what entails effective educational planning at all levels of education, taking into account political and cultural contexts. It also explores in-depth educational planning as it has been applied internationally within different milieus fostering a wide ranging understanding of the issue. In addition, current trends, practices and developments in educational planning have also been considered making the manual more up-to-date and relevant.

It is hoped that the erudition and insight of the book serve well for the readers.

Dr. R.K. Raghuram

Contents

1

National Policy on Education, 1986

Part I. Introductory

1.1 Education has continued to evolve, diversify and extend its reach and coverage since the dawn of human history. Every country develops its system of education to express and promote its unique sociocultural identity and also to meet the challenges of the times. There are moments in history when a new direction has to be given to an age-old process. That moment is today.

1.2 The country has reached a stage in its economic and technical development when a major effort must be made to derive the maximum benefit from the assets already created and to ensure that the fruits of change reach all sections. Education is the highway to that goal.

1.3 With this aim ill view, the Government of India announced in January 1985 that a new Education Policy would be formulated for the country. A comprehensive appraisal of the existing educational scene was made, followed by a countrywide debate. The views and suggestions received from different quarters were carefully studied.

The 1968 Education Policy and After

1.4 The National Policy of 1968 marked a significant step in the history of' education In post-independence India. It aimed to promote national progress, a sense, a sense of common citizenship and culture, and to strengthen national integration. It laid stress on the need for a radical reconstruction of the education system, to improve its quality at all stages, and gave much greater attention to science and technology, the cultivation of moral values and a closer relation between education and the life of the people.

1.5 Since the adoption of the 1968 policy, there has been considerable expansion in educational facilities all over the country at all levels. More than 90 per cent of the country's rural habitations now have schooling facilities within a radius of one kilometer. There has been sizable augmentation of facilities at other stages also.

1.6 Perhaps the most notable development has been the acceptance of a common structure of education throughout the country and the introduction on the 10 + 2 + 3 system by most States. In the school curricula, in addition to laying down a common scheme of studies for boys and girls, science and mathematics were incorporated as compulsory subjects and work experience assigned a place of importance.

1.7 A beginning was also made in restructuring of courses at the undergraduate level. Centres of Advanced Studies were set up for post-graduate education and research. And we have been able to meet our requirements of educated manpower.

1.8 While these achievements are impressive by themselves, the general formulations incorporated in the 1968 Policy did not, however, get translated into a detailed strategy of implementation, accompanied by the assignment of specific responsibilities and financial and organisational support. As a result, problems of access, quality, quantity, utility and financial outlay, accumulated over the years, have now assumed such massive proportions that they must be tackled with the utmost urgency.

1.9 Education in India stands at the cross roads today. Neither normal linear expansion nor the existing pace and nature of improvement can meet the needs of the situation.

1.10 In the Indian way of thinking, a human being is a positive asset and precious national resource which needs to he cherished, nurtured and developed with tenderness and care, coupled with dynamism. Each individual's growth presents a different range of problems and requirements, at every stage from the womb to the tomb. The catalytic action of education in this complex and dynamic growth process needs to be planned meticulously and executed with great sensitivity.

1.11 India's political and social life is passing through a phase which poses the danger of erosion to long-accepted values. The goals of secularism, socialism, democracy and professional ethics are coming under increasing strain.

1.12 The rural areas, with poor infrastructure and social services, will not get the benefit of trained and educated youth, unless rural-urban disparities are reduced and determined measures are taken to promote diversification and dispersal of employment opportunities.

1.13 The growth of our population needs to be brought down significantly order the coming decades. The largest single factor that could help to achieve this is the spread of literacy and education among women.

1.14 Life in the coming decades is likely to bring new tensions together with unprecedented opportunities. To enable the people to benefit in the new environment will require new designs of human resource development. The coming generations should have the ability to internalise new ideas constantly and creatively. They have to be imbued with a strong commitment to humane values and to social justice. All this implies better education.

1.15 Besides, a variety of new challenges and social needs make it imperative for the Government to formulate and implement a new Education Policy for the country. Nothing short of this will meet the situation.

Part II. The Essence and Role of Education

2.1 In our national perception education is essentially for all. This is fundamental to our all-round development, material and spiritual.

2.2 Education has an acculturating role. It refines sensitivities and perceptions that contribute to national cohesion, a scientific temper and independence of mind and spirit-thus furthering the goals of socialism, secularism and democracy enshrined in our Constitution.

2.3 Education develops manpower for different levels of the economy. It is also the substrata on which research and development flourish, being the ultimate guarantee of national self-reliance.

2.4 In sum, education is a unique investment in the present and file future. This cardinal principle is the key to the National Policy on Education.

Part III. National System of Education

3.1 The Constitution embodies the principles on which the National System of Education is conceived of.

3.2 The concept of a National System of Education implies that, tip to a given level, all students, irrespective of caste, creed, location or sex, have access to education of a comparable quality. To achieve this, the Government will initiate appropriately funded programmes. Effective measures will be taken in the direction of the Common School System recommended in the 1968 policy.

3.3 The National System of Education envisages a common educational structure. The 10+2+3 structure has now been accepted in all parts of the country. Regarding the further break-up of the first 10 years efforts will be made to move towards an elementary system comprising 5 years of primary education and 3 years of upper primary, followed by 2 years of high school.

3.4 The National System of Education will be based on a national curricular framework which contains a common core along with other components that are flexible. The common core will include the history of India's freedom movement, the constitutional obligations and other content essential to nurture national identity. These elements will cut across subject areas and will be designed to promote values such as India's common Cultural heritage, egalitarianism, democracy and secularism, equality of the sexes, protection of the environment, removal of social barriers, observance of the small family norm and inculcation of the scientific temper. All educational programmes will be carried on in strict conformity with secular values.

3.5 India has always worked for peace and understanding between nations, treating the whole world as one family. True to this hoary tradition, Education has to strengthen this world view and motivate the younger generations for international cooperation and peaceful coexistence. This aspect cannot be neglected.

3.6 To promote equality, it will be necessary to provide for equal opportunity to all not only in access, but also in the conditions for success. Besides, awareness of the inherent equality of all will be created through the core curriculum. The purpose is to remove prejudices and complexes transmitted through the social environment and the accident of birth.

3.7 Minimum levels of learning will be laid down for each stage of education. Steps will also be taken to foster among students an understanding of the diverse cultural and social systems of the people living in different parts of the country. Besides the promotion of the link language, programmes will also be launched to increase substantially the translation of books from one language to another and to publish multilingual dictionaries and glossaries. The young will be encouraged to undertake the rediscovery of India, each in his own image and perception.

3.8 In higher education in general, and technical education in particular, steps will be taken to facilitate inter-regional mobility by providing equal access to every Indian of requisite merit, regardless of his origins. The universal character of universities and other institutions of higher education is to be underscored.

3.9 In the areas of research and development, and education in science and technology, special measures will be taken to establish network arrangements between different institutions in the country to pool their resources and participate in projects of national importance.

3.10 The Nation as a whole will assume the responsibility of providing resource support for implementing programmes of educational transformation, reducing disparities, universalisation of elementary education, adult literacy, scientific and technological research, etc.

3.11 Life-long education is a cherished goal of the educational process. This presupposes universal literacy. Opportunities will be provided to the youth, housewives, agricultural and industrial workers and professionals to continue the education of their choice, at the pace suited to them. The future thrust will be in the direction of open and distance learning.

3.12 The institutions which will be strengthened to play an important role in giving shape to the National System of Education are the University Grants Commission, the All India Council of Technical Education, the Indian Council of Agricultural Research and the Indian Medical Council. Integrated planning will be instituted among all these bodies so as to establish functional linkages and reinforce programmes of research and postgraduate education. These, together with the National Council of Educational Research and Training, the National Institute of Educational Planning and Administration and the International Institute of Science and Technology Education will be involved in implementing the Education Policy.

A Meaningful Partnership

3.13 The Constitutional Amendment of 1976, which includes Education in the Concurrent List, was a far-reaching step whose implications—substantive, financial and administrative—require a new sharing of responsibility between the Union Government and the State in respect of this vital area of national life. While the role and responsibility of the States in regard to education will remain essentially unchanged, the Union Government would accept a larger responsibility to reinforce the national and integrative character of education, to maintain quality and standards (including those of the teaching profession at all levels), to study and monitor the educational requirements of the country, as a whole in regard to manpower for development, to cater to the needs of research and advanced study, to look after the international aspects of' education, culture and Human Resource Development and, in general, to promote excellence at all levels of the educational pyramid throughout the country. Concurrency signifies a partnership which is at once meaningful and challenging; the National Policy will be oriented towards giving effect to it in letter and spirit.

PART IV. EDUCATION FOR EQUALITY

Disparities

4.1 The new policy will lay special emphasis on the removal of disparities and to equalise educational opportunity by attending to the specific needs of those who have been denied equality so far.

Education For Women's Equality

4.2 Education will be used as an agent of basic change in the status of women. In order to neutralise the accumulated distortions of the past, there will be a well-conceived edge in favour of women. The

National Education System will play a positive, interventionist role in the empowerment of women. It will foster the development of new values through redesigned curricula, textbooks, the training and orientation of teachers, decision-makers and administrators, and the active involvement of educational institutions. This will be an act of faith and social engineering. Women's studies will be promoted as a part of various courses and educational institutions encouraged to take up active programmes to further women's development.

4.3 The removal of women's illiteracy and obstacles inhibiting their access to, and retention in, elementary education will receive overriding priority, through provision of special support services, setting of time targets, and effective monitoring. Major emphasis will be laid on women's participation in vocational, technical and professional education at different levels. The policy of non-discrimination will be pursued vigorously to eliminate sex stereotyping in vocational and professional courses and to promote women's participation in non-traditional occupations, as well as in existing and emergent technologies.

The Education of Scheduled Castes

4.4 The central focus in the SCs' educational development is their equalisation with the non-SC population at all stages and levels of education, in all areas and in all the four dimensions—rural male, rural female, urban male and urban females.

4.5 The measures contemplated for this purpose include:

i) Incentives to indigent families to send their children to school regularly till they reach the age of 14;

ii) Pre-matric scholarship scheme for children of families engaged in occupations such as scavenging, flaying and tanning to be made applicable from Class I onwards. All children of such families, regardless of incomes, will be covered by this scheme and time-bound programmes targeted on them will be undertaken;

iii) Constant micro-planning and verification to ensure that the enrolment, retention and successful completion of courses by SC students do not fall at any stage, and provision of remedial courses to improve their prospects for further education and employment.

iv) Recruitment of teachers from Scheduled Castes;

v) Provision of facilities for SC students in students' hostels at district headquarters, according to a phased programme;

vi) Location of school buildings, Balwadis and Adult Education Centres in such a way as to facilitate full participation of the Scheduled Castes;

vii) The utilisation of NREP and RLEGP resources so as to make substantial educational facilities available to the Scheduled Castes; and

viii) Constant innovation in finding new methods to increase the participation of the Scheduled Castes in the educational process.

The Education of Scheduled Tribes

4.6 The following measures will be taken urgently to bring the Scheduled Tribes on par with others:

i) Priority will be accorded to opening primary schools in tribal areas. The construction of school building will be undertaken in these areas on a priority basis under the normal funds for education, as well as under the NEEP, RLEGP, Tribal Welfare Schemes, etc.

ii) The socio-cultural milieu of the STs has its distinctive characteristics including, in many cases, their own spoken languages. This underlines the need to develop the curricula and devise instructional materials in tribal languages at the initial stages, with arrangements for switching over to the regional language.

iii) Educated and promising Scheduled Tribe youths will be encouraged and trained to take up teaching in tribal areas.

iv) Residential schools, including Ashram Schools, will be established on a large scale.

v) Incentive schemes will be formulated for the Scheduled Tribes, keeping in view their special needs and life styles. Scholarships for higher education will emphasise technical, professional and para-professional courses. Special remedial courses and other programmes to remove psycho-social impediments will be provided to improve their performances in various courses.

vi) Anganwadis, Non-formal and Adult Education Centres will be opened on a priority basis in areas predominantly inhabited by the Scheduled Tribes.

vii) The curriculum at all stages of education will be designed to create an awareness of the rich cultural identity of the tribal people as also of their enormous creative talent.

Other Educationally Backward Sections and Areas

4.7 Suitable incentives will be provided to all educationally backward sections of society, particularly in the rural areas. Hill and desert districts, remote and inaccessible areas and islands will be provided adequate institutional infrastructure.

Minorities

4.8 Some minority groups are educationally deprived or backward. Greater attention will be paid to the education of these groups in the interests of equality and social justice. This will naturally include the Constitutional guarantees given to them to establish and administer their own educational institutions, and protection to their languages and culture. Simultaneously, objectivity will be reflected in the, preparation of textbooks and in all school activities, and all possible measures will be taken to promote an integration based on appreciation of common national goals and ideals, in conformity with the core curriculum.

The Handicapped

4.9 The objective should be to integrate the physically and mentally handicapped with the general community as equal partners, to prepare them for normal growth and to enable them to face life with courage and confidence. The following measures will be taken in this regard:

i) Wherever it is feasible, the education of children with motor handicaps and other mild handicaps will be common with that of others.

ii) Special schools with hostels will be provided, as far as possible at district headquarters, for the severely handicapped children.

iii) Adequate arrangements will be made to give vocational training to the disabled.

iv) Teacher's training programme will be re-oriented, in particular for teachers of primary classes, to deal with the special difficulties of the handicapped children; and

v) Voluntary effort for the education of the disabled will be encouraged in every possible manner.

Adult Education

4.10 Our ancient scriptures define education as that which liberates i.e., provides the instruments for liberation from ignorance and oppression. In the modern world, it would naturally include the ability to read and write, since that is the main instrument of learning. Hence the crucial importance of adult education, including adult literacy.

4.11 The critical development issue today is the continuous upgradation of skills so as to produce manpower resources of the kind and the number required by the society. Since participation by beneficiaries in the development programmes is of crucial importance, systematic programmes of adult education linked with national goals such as alleviation of poverty, national integration, environmental conservation, energisation of the cultural creativity of the people, observance of small family norm, promotion of women's equality, etc. will be organised and the existing programmes reviewed and strengthened.

4.12 The whole nation must pledge itself to the eradication of illiteracy, particularly in the 15-35 age group. The Central and State Governments, political parties and their mass organisations, the mass media and educational institutions must commit themselves to mass literacy programmes of diverse nature. It will also have to involve on a large scale teachers, students, youth, voluntary agencies, employers, etc. Concerted efforts will be made to harness various research agencies to improve the pedagogical aspects of adult literacy. The mass literacy programme would include, in addition to literacy, functional knowledge and skills, and also awareness among learners about the socio-economic reality and the possibility to change it.

4.13 A vast programme of adult and continuing education will be implemented through various ways and channels, including:

a) establishment of centres in rural areas for continuing education;

b) workers' education through the employers, trade unions and concerned agencies of government;

c) post-secondary education institutions;

d) wider promotion of books, libraries and reading rooms;

e) use of radio, TV and films, as mass and group learning media;

f) creation of learners' groups and organisations;

g) programmes of distance learning;

h) organising assistance in self-learning; and

i) organising need and interest-based vocational training programmes.

PART V. Reorganisation of Education at Different Stages

Early Childhood Care and Education

5.1 The National Policy on Children specially emphasises investment in the development of the young child, particularly children from sections of the population in which first generation learners predominate.

5.2 Recognising the holistic nature of child development, viz., nutrition, health and social, mental, physical, moral and emotional development, Early Childhood Care and Education (ECCE) will receive high priority and be suitably integrated with the Integrated Child Development Services Programme, wherever possible. Day-care centres will be provided as a support service for universalisation of primary education, to enable girls engaged in taking care of siblings to attend school and as a support service for working women belonging to poorer sections.

5.3 Programmes of ECCE will be child-oriented, focused around play and the individuality of the child. Formal methods and introduction of the 3R's will be discouraged at this stage. The local community will be fully involved in these programmes.

5.4 A full integration of child care and pre-primary education will be brought about, both as a feeder and a strengthening factor for primary education and for human resource development in general. In continuation of this stage, the School Health Programme will be strengthened.

Elementary Education

5.5 The new thrust in elementary education will emphasise two aspects: (i) universal enrolment and universal retention of children up to 14 years of age, and (ii) a substantial improvement in the quality of education.

Child-Centred Approach

5.6 A warm, welcoming and encouraging approach, in which all concerned share a solicitude for the needs of the child, is the best motivation for the child to attend school and learn. A child-centred and activity-based process of learning should be adopted at the primary stage. First generation allowed to set their own pace and be given supplementary remedial instruction. As the child grows, the component of cognitive learning will be increased and skills organised through practice. The policy of non-detention at the primary stage will be retained, making evaluation as disaggregated as feasible. Corporal punishment will be firmly excluded from the educational system and school timings as well as vacations adjusted to the convenience of children.

School Facilities

5.7 Provision will be made of essential facilities in primary schools, including at least two reasonably large rooms that are usable in all weather, and the necessary toys, blackboards, maps, charts, and other learning material. At least two teachers, one of whom a woman, should work in every school, the number increasing as early as possible to one teacher per class. A phased drive, symbolically called Operation Blackboard will be undertaken with immediate effect to improve primary schools all over the country. Government, local bodies, voluntary agencies and individuals will be fully involved. Construction of school buildings will be the first charge on NREP and RLEGP funds.

Non-Formal Education

5.8 A large and systematic programme of non-formal education will be launched for school drop-outs, for children from habitations without schools, working children and girls who cannot attend whole-day schools.

5.9 Modern technological aids will be used to improve the learning environment of NFE centres. Talented and dedicated young men and women from the local community will be chosen to serve as instructors, and particular attention paid to their training. Steps will be taken to facilitate their entry into the formal system in deserving cases. All necessary measures will be taken to ensure that the quality of non-formal education is comparable with formal education.

5.10 Effective steps will be taken to provide a framework for the curriculum on the lines of the national core curriculum, but based on the needs of the learners and related to the local environment. Learning material of high quality will be developed and provided free of charge to all pupils. NFE programmes will provide participatory learning environment, and activities such as games and sports, cultural programmes, excursions, etc.

5.11 Much of the work of running NFE centres will be done through voluntary agencies and panchayati raj institutions. The provision of funds to these agencies will be adequate and timely. The Government will take over-all responsibility for this vital sector.

A Resolve

5.12 The new education policy will give the highest

priority to solving the problem of' children dropping out of school and will adopt an array of meticulously formulated strategies based on micro-planning, and applied at the grass-roots level all over the country, to ensure children's retention at school. This effort will be fully coordinated with the network of non-formal education. It shall be ensured that all children who attain the age of about 11 years by 1990 will have had five years of schooling, or its equivalent through the non-formal stream. Likewise, by 1995 all children will be provided free and compulsory education upto 14 years of age.

Secondary Education

5.13 Secondary education begins to expose students to the differentiated roles of science, the humanities and social sciences. This is also an appropriate stage to provide children with a sense of history and national perspective and give them opportunities to understand their constitutional duties and rights as citizens. Conscious internalisation of a healthy work ethos and of the values of a humane and composite culture will be brought about through appropriately formulated curricula. Vocationalisation through specialised institutions or through the refashioning of secondary education can, at this stage, provide valuable manpower for economic growth. Access to secondary education will be widened to cover areas unserved by it at present. In other areas, the main emphasis will be on consolidation.

5.14 It is universally accepted that children with special talent or aptitude should be provided opportunities to proceed at a faster pace, by making good quality education available to them, irrespective of their capacity to pay for it.

5.15 Pace-setting schools intended to serve this purpose will be established in various parts of the country on a given pattern, but with full scope for innovation and experimentation. Their broad aims will be to serve the objective of excellence, coupled with equity and social justice (with reservation for SCs and STs), to promote national integration by providing opportunities to talented children largely rural, from different parts of the country to live and learn together, to develop their full potential, and, most importantly, to become catalysts of a nation-wide programme of school improvement. The schools will be residential and free of charge.

Vocationalisation

5.16 The introduction of systematic, well-planned and rigorously implemented programmes of vocational education is crucial in the proposed educational reorganisation. These elements are meant to enhance individual employability, to reduce the mismatch between the demand and supply of skilled manpower, and to provide an alternative for those pursuing higher education without particular interest or purpose.

5.17 Vocational education will be a distinct stream, intended to prepare students for identified occupations spanning several areas of activity. These courses will ordinarily be provided after the secondary stage, but keeping the scheme flexible, they may also be made available after Class VIII. In the interests of integrating vocational education better with their facilities the Industrial Training Institutes will also conform to the larger vocational pattern.

5.18 Health planning and health service management should optimally interlock with the education and training of appropriate categories of health manpower through health-related vocational courses. Health education at the primary and middle levels will ensure the commitment of the individual to family and community health, and lead to health-related vocational courses at the +2 stage of higher secondary education. Efforts will be made to devise similar vocational courses based on agriculture, marketing, social services etc. An emphasis in vocational education will also be on development of attitudes, knowledge, and skills for entrepreneurship and sell-employment.

5.19 The establishment of vocational courses or institutions will be the responsibility of the Government as well as employers in the public and private sectors; the Government will, however, take special steps to cater to the needs of women, rural and tribal students and the deprived sections of society. Appropriate programmes will also be started for the handicapped.

5.20 Graduates of vocational courses will be given opportunities, under predetermined conditions, for professional growth, career improvement and lateral entry into courses of general, technical and professional education through appropriate bridge courses.

5.21 Non-formal, flexible and need-based vocational programmes will also be made available to neoliterates, youth who have completed primary education, school drop-outs, persons engaged in work and unemployed or partially employed persons. Special attention in this regard will be given to women.

5.22 Tertiary level courses will be organised for the young who graduate from the higher secondary courses of the academic stream and may also require vocational courses.

5.23 It is proposed that vocational courses cover 10 per cent of higher secondary students by 1990 and 25 per cent by 1995. Steps will be taken to see that a substantial majority of the products of vocational courses are employed or become self-employed. Review of the courses offered would be regularly undertaken. Government will also review its recruitment policy to encourage diversifications at the secondary level.

Higher Education

5.24 Higher education provides people with an opportunity to reflect on the critical social, economic, cultural, moral and spiritual issues facing humanity. It contributes to national development through dissemination of specialised knowledge and skills. It is therefore a crucial factor for survival. Being at the apex of the educational pyramid, it has also a key role in producing teachers for the education system.

5.25 In the context of the unprecedented explosion of knowledge, higher education has to become dynamic as never before, constantly entering uncharted areas.

5.26 There are around 150 universities and about 5,000 colleges in India today. In view of the need to effect an all round improvement in these institutions, it is proposed that, in the near future, the main emphasis will be on the consolidation of, and expansion of facilities in, the existing institutions.

5.27 Urgent steps will be taken to protect the system from degradation.

5.28 In view of mixed experiences with the system of affiliation autonomous colleges will be helped to develop in large numbers until the affiliating system is replaced by a freer and more creative association of universities with colleges. Similarly, the creation of autonomous departments within universities on a selective basis will be encouraged. Autonomy and freedom will be accompanied by accountability.

5.29 Course and programmes will be redesigned to meet the demands of specialisation better. Special emphasis will be laid on linguistic competence. There will be increasing flexibility in the combination of courses.

5.30 State level planning and coordination of higher education will be done through Councils of Higher Education. The UGC and these Councils will develop coordinative methods to keep a watch on standards.

5.31 Provision will be made for minimum facilities and admission will be regulated according to capacity. A major effort will be directed towards the transformation of' teaching methods. Audio-visual aids and electronic equipment will be introduced; development of science and technology curricula and material, research, and teacher orientation will receive attention. This will require preparation of teachers at the beginning of the service as well as continuing education thereafter. Teacher's performance will be systematically assessed. All posts will be filled on the basis of merit.

5.32 Research in the universities will be provided enhanced support and steps will be taken to ensure its high quality. Suitable mechanisms will be set up by the UGC for coordinating research in the universities, particularly in thrust areas of science and technology, with research undertaken by other agencies. An effort will be made to encourage the setting up of national research facilities within the university system, with proper forms of autonomous management.

5.33 Research in Indology, the humanities and social sciences will receive adequate support. To fulfil the need for the synthesis of knowledge, inter-disciplinary research will be encouraged. Efforts will be made to delve into India's ancient fund of knowledge and to relate it to contemporary reality. This effort will imply the development of facilities for the intensive study of Sanskrit and other classical language.

5.40 De-linking will be applied in services university degree need not be a necessary qualification. Its implementation will lead to a re-fashioning of job-specific courses and afford greater justice to those candidates who, despite being equipped for a given job, are unable to get it because of it is unnecessary for graduate candidates.

5.41 Concomitant with de-linking, an appropriate machinery, such as a National Testing Service, will be established, in appropriate phases, to conduct tests on a voluntary basis to determine the suitability of candidates for specified jobs and to pave the way for the emergence of norms of comparable competence across the nation.

Part VI. Technical And Management Education

6.3 In order to improve the situation regarding manpower information, the recently set up Technical Manpower Information System will be further developed and strengthened.

6.4 Continuing education, covering established as well as emerging technologies, will be promoted.

6.5 As computers have become important and ubiquitous tools, a minimal exposure to computers and a training in their use will form part of professional education. Programmes of computer literacy will be organised on wide scale from the school stage.

6.6 In view of the present rigid entry requirements to formal courses restricting the access of a large segment of people to technical and managerial education, programmes through a distance-learning process, including uses of the mass media, will be offered. Technical and management education programmes, including education in polytechnics, will also be on a flexible modular pattern based, on credits, with provision for multi-point entry. A strong guidance and counselling service will be provided.

6.7 In order to increase the relevance of management education, particularly in the non-corporate and under-managed sectors, the management education system will study and document the Indian experience and create a body of knowledge and specific educational programmes suited to these sectors.

6.8 Appropriate formal and non-formal programmes of technical education will be devised for the benefit of women, the economically and socially weaker sections, and the physically handicapped.

6.9 The emphasis on vocational education and its expansion will need a large number of teachers and professionals in vocational education, educational technology curriculum development, etc. Programmes will be started to meet this demand.

6.10 To encourage students to consider 'self-employment' as a career option, training in entrepreneurship will be provided through modular of optional courses, in degree or diploma programmes.

6.11 In order to meet the continuing needs of updating curriculum, renewal should systematically phase out obsolescence and introduce new technologies or disciplines.

Institutional Thrusts

6.12 Some polytechnics in the rural areas have started training weaker groups in those areas for productive occupations through a system of community polytechnics. The community polytechnic system will be appraised and appropriately strengthened to increase its quality and coverage.

Innovation, Research and Development

6.13 Research as a means of renovation and renewal of educational processes will be undertaken by all higher technical institutions. It will primarily aim at producing quality manpower capable of taking tip R&D functions. Research for development will focus on improving present technologies, developing new indigenous ones and enhancing production and productivity. A suitable system for watching and forecasting technology will be set up.

6.14 The scope for cooperation, collaboration and networking relationships between institutions at various levels and with the user systems will be utilised. Proper maintenance and an attitude of innovation and improvement will be promoted systematically.

Promoting Efficiency and Effectiveness at All Levels

6.15 As technical and management education is expensive, the following major steps will be taken for cost-effectiveness and to promote excellence:

i) High priority will be given to modernisation and removal of obsolescence. However, modernisation will be undertaken to enhance functional efficiency and not for its own sake or as a status symbol;

ii) Institutions will be encouraged to generate resources using their capacities to provide services to the community and industry. They will be equipped with up-to-date learning resources, library and computer facilities;

iii) Adequate hostel accommodation will be provided, specially for girls. Facilities for sports, creative work and cultural activities will be expanded;

iv) More effective procedures will be adopted in the recruitment of staff. Career opportunities, service conditions, consultancy norms and other perquisites will be improved.

v) Teachers will have multiple roles to perform: teaching, research, development of learning resource material, extension, and managing the institution. Initial and in-service training will be made mandatory for faculty members and adequate training reserves will be provided. Staff Development Programmes will be integrated at the State, and coordinated at regional and national levels.

vi) The curricula of technical and management programmes will be targeted on current as well as the projected needs of industry or user system. Active interaction between technical or management institutions and industry will be promoted in programme planning and implementation, exchange of personnel, training facilities and resources, research and consultancy and other areas of mutual interest.

vii) Excellence in performance of institutions and individuals will be recognised and rewarded. The emergence of substandard and institutions will be checked. A climate conducive to excellence and innovation will be promoted with full involvement of the faculty.

viii) Select institutions will be awarded academic administrative and financial autonomy of varying degrees, building in safeguards with respect to accountability.

ix) Networking systems will have to be established between technical education and industry, R&D organisations, programmes of rural and community development, and with other sectors of education with complementary characteristics.

Management Functions and Change

6.16 In view of the likely emergence of changes in management systems and the need to equip students with the ability to cope with them, effective mechanisms will be devised to understand the nature and direction of changes *per se* and to develop the important skill of managing change.

6.17 In view of the integrated nature of the task, the Ministry of Human Resource Development will coordinate the balanced development of engineering, vocational and management education as well as the education of technicians and craftsmen.

6.18 Professional societies will be encouraged and enabled to perform their due role in the advancement of technical and management education.

6.19 The All India Council for Technical Education will be vested with statutory authority for planning, formulation and the maintenance of norms and standards, accreditation, funding of priority areas, monitoring and evaluation, maintaining parity of certification and awards and ensuring the coordinated and integrated development of technical and management education. Mandatory periodic evaluation will be carried out by a duty constituted Accreditation Board.

6.20 In the interests of maintaining standards and for several other valid reasons, the commercialisation of technical and professional education will be curbed. An alternative system will be devised to involve private and voluntary effort in this sector of education, in conformity with accepted norms and goals.

Part VII. Making the System Work

7.1 It is obvious that these and many other new tasks of education cannot be performed in a state of disorder. Education needs to be managed in an atmosphere of utmost intellectual rigour, seriousness of purpose and, at the same time, of freedom essential for innovation and creativity. While far-reaching change will have to be incorporated in the quality and range of education, the process of introducing discipline into the system will have to be started, here and now, in what exists.

7.2 The country has placed boundless trust in the educational system. The people have a right to expect concrete results. The first task is to make it work. All teachers should teach and all students study.

7.3 The strategy in this behalf will consist of:

a) a better deal to teachers with greater accountability;

b) provision of improved student's services and

insistence on observance of acceptable norms of behaviour;

c) provision of better facilities to institutions; and

d) creation of a system of performance appraisals of institutions according to standards and norms set at the national or state levels.

PART VIII. REORIENTING THE CONTENT AND PROCESS OF EDUCTION

The Cultural Perspective

8.1 The existing schism between the formal system of education and the country's rich and varied cultural traditions needs to be bridged. The preoccupation with modern technologies cannot be allowed to sever out new generations from the roots in India's history and culture. De-culturisation, de-humanisation and alienation must be avoided at all costs. Education can and must bring about the fine synthesis between change-oriented technologies and the country's continuity of cultural tradition.

8.2 The curricula and processes of education will be enriched by cultural content in as many manifestations as possible. Children will be enabled to develop sensitivity to beauty, harmony and refinement. Resource persons in the community, irrespective of their formal educational qualifications, will be invited to contribute to the cultural enrichment of education, employing both the literate oral traditions of communication. To sustain and carry forward the cultural tradition, the role of old masters, who train pupils through traditional modes will be supported and recognised.

8.3 Linkages will be established between the university system and institutions of higher learning in art, archaeology, oriental studies etc. Due attention will also be paid to the specialised disciplines of fine arts, museology, folklore, etc. Teaching, training and research in these disciplines will be strengthened so as to replenish specialised manpower in them.

Value Education

8.4 The growing concern over the erosion of essential values and an increasing cynicism in society has brought to focus the need for readjustments in the curriculum in order to make education a forceful tool for the cultivation of social and moral values.

8.5 In our culturally plural society, education should foster universal and internal values oriented towards the unity and integration of our people. Such value education should help eliminate obscurantism, religious fanaticism, violence, superstition and fatalism.

8.6 Apart from this combative role, value education has a profound positive content, based on our heritage, national goals universal perceptions. It should lay primary emphasis on this aspect.

Languages

8.7 The education policy of 1968 had examined the question of the development of languages in great detail; its essential provisions can hardly be improved upon and are as relevant today as before. The implementation of this part of the 1968 policy has, however, been uneven. The policy will be implemented more energetically and purposefully.

Books and Libraries

8.8 The availability of books at low prices is

indispensable for people's education. Effort will be made to secure easy accessibility to books for all segments of the population. Measures will be taken to improve the quality of books, promote the reading habit and encourage creative writing. Authors' interests will be protected. Good translations of foreign books into Indian languages will be supported. Special attention will be paid to the production of quality books for children, including text books and work books.

8.9 Together with the development of books, a nation-wide movement for the improvement of existing libraries and the establishment of new ones will be taken up. Provision will be made in all educational institutions for library facilities and the status of librarians improved.

Media and Educational Technology

8.10 Modern communication technologies have the potential to bypass several stages and sequences in the process of development encountered in earlier decades. Both the constraints of time and distance at once become manageable. In order to avoid structural dualism, modern educational technology must reach out to the most distant areas and the most deprived sections of beneficiaries simultaneously with the areas of comparative affluence and ready availability.

8.11 Educational technology will be employed in the spread of useful information, the training and re-training of teachers, to improve quality, sharpen awareness of art and culture, inculcate abiding values, etc., both in the formal and non-formal sectors. Maximum use will be made of the available infrastructure. In villages without electricity, batteries or solar packs will be used to run the programme.

8.12 The generation of relevant and culturally compatible educational programmes will form an important component of educational technology, and all available resources in the country will be utilised for this purpose.

8.13 The media have a profound influence on the minds of children as well as adults; some of them tend to encourage consumerism, violence, etc., and have a deleterious effect. Radio and TV programmes which clearly militate against proper educational objectives will be prevented. Steps will be taken to discourage such trends in films and other media also. An active movement will be started to promote the production of children's films of high quality and usefulness.

Work Experience

8.14 Work experience, viewed as purposive and meaningful manual work, organised as an integral part of the learning process and resulting in either goods or services useful to the community, is considered as an essential component at all stages of education, to be provided through well-structured and graded programmes. It would comprise activities in accord with the interests, abilities and needs of students, the level of skills and knowledge to be upgraded with the stages of education. This experience would be helpful on his entry into the workforce. Pre-vocational programmes provided at the lower secondary stage will also facilitate the choice of the vocational courses at the higher secondary stage.

Education and Environment

8.15 There is a paramount need to create a consciousness of the environment. It must permeate all ages and all sections of society, beginning with the child.

Environmental consciousness should inform teaching in schools and colleges. This aspect will be integrated in the entire educational process.

Mathematics Teaching

8.16 Mathematics should be visualised as the vehicle to train a child to think, reason, analyse and to articulate logically. Apart from being a specific subject, it should be treated as a concomitant to any subject involving analysis and reasoning.

8.17 With the recent introduction of computers in schools, educational computing and the emergence of learning through the understanding of cause-effect relationships and the interplay of variables, the teaching of mathematics will be suitably redesigned to bring it in line with modern technological devices.

Science Education

8.18 Science education will be strengthened so as to develop in the child well defined abilities and values such as the spirit of inquiry, creativity, objectivity, the courage to question, and an aesthetic sensibility.

8.19 Science education programmes will be designed to enable the learner to acquire problem-solving and decision-making skills and to discover the relationship of science with health, agriculture, industry and other aspects of daily life. Every effort will be made to extend science education to the vast numbers who have remained outside the pale of formal education.

Sports and Physical Education

8.20 Sports and physical education are an integral part of the learning process, and will be included in the evaluation of performance. A nation-wide infrastructure for physical education, sports and games will be built into the educational edifice.

8.21 The infrastructure will consist of playfields, equipment, coaches and teachers of physical education as part of the school improvement programme. Available open spaces in urban areas will be reserved for playgrounds, if necessary by legislation. Efforts will be made to establish sports institutions and hostels where specialised attention will be given to sports activities and sports-related studies, along with normal education. Appropriate encouragement will be given to those talented in sport and games. Due stress will be laid on indigenous traditional games. As a system which promotes an integrated development of body and mind, yoga will receive special attention. Efforts will be made to introduce yoga in all schools; to this end, it will be introduced in teacher training courses.

The Role of Youth

8.22 Opportunities will be provided for the youth to involve themselves in national and social development through educational institutions and outside them. Students will be required to participate in one or the other of existing schemes, namely, the National Service Scheme, National Cadet Corps, etc. Outside the institutions, the youth will be encouraged to take up programmes of development, reform and extension. The National Service Volunteer Scheme will be strengthened.

The Evaluation Process and Examination Reform

8.23 Assessment of performance is an integral part of any process of learning and teaching. As part of sound educational strategy, examinations should be employed to bring about qualitative improvements in education.

8.24 The objective will be to re-cast the examination system so as to ensure a method of assessment that is a valid and reliable measure of student development and a powerful instrument for improving teaching and learning. In functional terms, this would mean:

i) The elimination of excessive element of chance and subjectivity;

ii) The de-emphasis of memorisation;

iii) Continuous and comprehensive evaluation that incorporates both scholastic and non-scholastic aspects of education, spread over the total span of instructional time;

iv) Effective use of the evaluation process by teachers, students and parents:

v) Improvement in the conduct of examinations;

vi) The introduction of concomitant changes in instructional materials and methodology;

vii) Introduction of the semester system from the secondary stage in a phased manner; and

viii) The use of grades in place of marks.

8.25 The above goals are relevant both for external examinations and evaluation within educational institutions. Evaluation at the institutional level will be streamlined and the predominance of external examinations reduced.

PART IX. THE TEACHER

9.1 The status of the teacher reflects the socio-cultural ethos of a society; it is said that no people can rise above the level of its teachers. The Government and the community should endeavour to create conditions which will help motivate and inspire teachers on constructive and creative lines. Teachers should have the freedom to innovate, to devise appropriate methods of communication and activities relevant to the needs and capabilities of and the concerns of the community.

9.2 The methods of recruiting teachers will be reorganised to ensure merit, objectivity and conformity with spatial and functional requirements. The pay and service conditions of teachers have to be commensurate with their social and professional responsibilities and with the need to attract talent to the profession. Efforts will be made to reach the desirable objective of uniform emoluments, service conditions and grievance-removal mechanisms for throughout the country. Guidelines will be formulated to ensure objectivity in the postings and transfers of teachers. A system of teacher evaluation—open, participative and data-based—will be created and reasonable opportunities of promotion to higher grades provided. Norms of accountability will be laid down with incentives for good performance and disincentives for non-performance. Teachers will continue to play a crucial role in the formulation and implementation of educational programmes.

9.3 Teachers' associations must play a significant role in upholding professional integrity, enhancing the dignity of the teacher and in curbing professional misconduct. National level associations of teachers, could prepare a Code of Professional Ethics for Teachers and see to its observance.

Teacher Education

9.4 Teacher education is a continuous process, and its pre-service and in-service components are inseparable. As the first step, the system of teacher education will be overhauled.

9.5 The new programmes of teacher-education will emphasise continuing education and the need for teachers to meet the thrusts envisaged in this policy.

9.6 District. Institutes of Education and Training (DIET) will be established with the capability to organise pre-service and in-service courses for elementary school teachers and for the personnel working in non-formal and adult education. As DIETs get established, substandard institutions will be phased out. Selected Secondary Teacher Training Colleges will be upgraded to complement the work of State Councils of Educational Research and Training. The National Council of Teacher Education will be provided the necessary resources and capability to accredit institutions of teacher-education and provide guidance regarding curricula and methods. Networking arrangements will be created between institutions of teacher education and university departments of education.

Part X. The Management of Education

10.1 An overhaul of the system of planning and the management of education will receive high priority. The guiding considerations will be:

a) Evolving a long-term planning and management perspective of education and its integration with the country's developmental and manpower needs;

b) Decentralisation and the creation of a spirit of autonomy for educational institutions;

c) Giving pre-eminence to people's involvement, including association of non-governmental agencies and voluntary effort;

d) Inducting more women in the planning and management of education; and

e) Establishing the principle of accountability in relation to given objectives and norms.

National Level

10.2 The Central Advisory Board of Education will play a pivotal rote in reviewing educational development, determining the changes required to improve the system and monitoring implementation. It will function through appropriate committees and other mechanisms created to ensure contact with, and co-ordination among, the various areas of human resource development. The departments of education at the centre and in the states will be strengthened through the involvement of professionals.

Indian Education Service

10.3 A proper management structure in education will entail the establishment of the Indian Education Service as an All-India Service. It will bring a national perspective to this vital sector. The basic principles, functions and procedures of recruitment to this service will be decided in consultation with the State Governments.

State Level

10.4 State Governments may establish State Advisory Boards of Education on the lines of CABE. Effective measures should be taken to integrate mechanisms in the various State departments concerned with Human Resource Development.

10.5 Special attention will be paid to the training of educational planners, administrators and heads of institutions. Institutional arrangements for this purpose should be set up in stages.

District and Local Level

10.6 District Boards of Education will be created to manage education up to the higher secondary level. State Governments will attend to this aspect with all possible expedition. Within a multi-level framework of educational development, central, state, district and local level agencies will participate in planning, coordination, monitoring and evaluation.

10.7 A very important role must be assigned to the head of an educational institution. Heads will be specially selected and trained. School complexes will be promoted on a flexible pattern so as to serve as networks of institutions and synergic alliances to encourage professionalism among teachers, to ensure observance of norms of conduct and to enable the sharing of experiences and facilities. It is expected that a developed system of school complexes will take much of the inspection functions in due course.

10.8 Local communities, through appropriate bodies, will be assigned a major role in programmes of school improvement.

Voluntary Agencies and Aided Institutions

10.9 Non-government and voluntary effort including social activist groups will be encouraged, subject to proper management, and financial assistance provided. At the same time, steps will be taken to prevent the establishment of institutions set up to commercialise education.

PART XI. RESOURCES AND REVIEW

11.1 The Education Commission of 1964-66, the National Education Policy of 1968 and practically all others concerned with education have stressed that the egalitarian goals and the practical, development-oriented objectives of Indian society can be realised only by making investments in education of an order commensurate with the nature and dimensions of the task.

11.2 Resources, to the extent possible, will be raised by mobilising donations, asking the beneficiary communities to maintain school buildings and supplies of some consumables, raising fees at the higher levels of education and effecting some savings by the efficient use of facilities. Institutions involved with research and the development of technical and scientific manpower should also mobilise some funds by levying access or charge on the user agencies, including government departments, and entrepreneurs. All these measures will be taken not only to reduce the burden on State resources but also for creating a greater sense of responsibility within the educational system. However, such measures will contribute only marginally to the total funding. The government and the community in general will find funds for such programmes as: the universalisation of elementary education; liquidating illiteracy; equality of access to educational opportunities to all sections throughout the country; enhancing the social relevance, quality and functional effectiveness of educational programmes; generating knowledge and developing technologies in scientific fields crucial to self-sustaining economic development; and creating a critical consciousness of the values and imperatives of national survival.

11.3 The deleterious consequences of non-investment or inadequate investment in education are indeed very serious. Similarly, the cost of neglecting vocational and technical education and of research is also unacceptable. Sub-optimal performance in these fields could cause irreparable damage to the Indian economy. The network of institutions set up from time to time since independence to facilitate the application of science and technology would need to be substantially and expeditiously updated, since they are fast becoming obsolete.

11.4 In view of these imperatives, education will be treated as a crucial area of investment for national development and survival. The National Policy on Education, 1968, had laid down that the investment on education be gradually increased to reach a level of expenditure of 6 per cent of the national income as early as possible. Since the actual level of investment has remained far short of that target, it is important that greater determination be shown now to find the funds for the programmes laid down in this policy. While the actual requirements will be computed from time to time on the basis of monitoring and review, the outlay on education will be shaped up to the extent essential for policy implementation in the Seventh Plan. It will be ensured that from the Eighth Five Year Plan onwards it will uniformly exceed to 6 per cent of the national income.

Review

11.5 The implementation of the various parameters of the new policy must be reviewed every five years. Appraisals at short intervals will also be made to ascertain the progress of implementation and the trends emerging from time to time.

PART XII. THE FUTURE

12.1 The future of education in India is too complex to envision with precision. Yet, given our tradition which has almost always put a high premium on intellectual and spiritual attainment, we are bound to succeed in achieving our objectives.

12.2 The main tasks is to strengthen the base of the pyramid, which might come close to a billion people at the turn of the century. Equally, it is important to ensure that those at the top of the pyramid are among the best in the world. Our cultural wellsprings had taken good care of both ends in the past; the skew set in with foreign domination and influence. It should now be possible to further intensify the nation-wide effort in Human Resource Development, with education playing its multifaceted role.

2

National Policy on Education (NPE): Programme of Action

EARLY CHILDHOOD CARE AND EDUCATION

The Present Situation

1. Some of the significant parameters of the quality of life of any nation are the infant mortality rate, incidence of malnutrition, the morbidity picture and the literacy rates. The infant mortality rate today stands at 104 (1984). The rural-urban IMR differential is striking, being 113 and 66. Respiratory disorders, diarrhoea and parasitic infestations and nitritional deficiencies are significant contributors of child morbidity. Eighty-three per cent of children have body weights below normal standards. These include 42 per cent mildly malourished, 35 per cent moderately malnourished and six per cent severely malnourished. Cognitive stimulation at home during early childhood, which is so vital for the later years of life, is poor because of low female literacy rate which is 24.88. At present, by population (0-6 years) of the country is being reached by one or more of the six services in the ICDS package, through within ICDS project areas, a large proportion of disadvantaged children are benefited by the comprehensive package

of six services. Taking into account the various other programmes cater to differently defined age group (mostly 3-6), it appears that less than 10 per cent of the child population (0-6 years) of the country receives all the essential services, from conception to the age of 6 years.

2. Realising the crucial importance of rapid physical and mental growth during early childhood, Government started a number of programmes of early childhood care and education (ECCE). Declaration of a National Policy for Children (1974) shows the commitment of Govern-ment of the development of children. The existing ECCE programmes include:

   i) Integrated Child Development Services (ICDS);
   ii) Scheme of assistance to voluntary organisations for conducting early childhood education centres (ECE);
   iii) Balwadis and day-care centres run by voluntary agencies with Government's assistance;
   iv) Pre-primary schools run by the state Governments, Municipal Corporations and other agencies;
   v) Material and child health services through primary health centres and sub-centres and other agencies.

The Integrated Child Development Services is currently the biggest programme of early childhood development. This programme over the years has demonstrated that even a modest investment in child development goes a long way in developing human resources. It needs to be fully integrated with the Universal Immunisation Programme started with effect from 19th November, 1985.

3. The National Policy on Education has given a great deal of importance to ECCE. It views ECCE as an important input in the strategy of human resource development as a feeder and support programme for primary education and as a support service for working women of the disadvantaged sections of society. It has also taken into account the holistic nature of ECCE and has pointed out the need for organising programmes for the all-round development of the child. The significance of play and activity approach and the need for child-centredness in the programmes of ECCE as well as primary school education have been spelt out, and it cautions against the dangers of using formal methods of leaching and early introducing of the 3R's. The importance of community involvement has also been highlighted. The need to establish a linkage between ICDS and ECCE programmes has been pointed out. The desirability of a modular development so as to upgrade the former into the latter institution on a full-blown basis has been mentioned. In addition, there is also a commitment to taking up other diverse kinds of day-care centres. The Policy specifically focuses on the need for early care and stimulation of children belonging to the poverty groups.

The Strategy of Implementation

4. The ECCE involves the total development of child, i.e., physical, motor, cognitive, language, emotional, social and moral. The age span under consideration in ECCE is from conception to about 6 years. Thus, ECCE is a complex integral function. It requires workers with integrated ECCE training, integrated worksites or ECCE enters where the essential services flow to young children through the period of their

growth and preparation for formal education, and coordinated functioning of various agencies, governmental and non-governmental, striving to meet different needs of young children.

5. One of the weakest points in the existing programmes is inadequate child: worker ratio. Efforts will be made to strengthen the programmes and make them developmental instead of providing mere custodial care, the worker force would need to be suitably augmented. The size and personnel of the centre would be so chosen that it would take care of the diverse items of the programmes fully within a given population.

6. Similarly, adequate remuneration to the workers is an important factor in successful implementation of any programme. Effort will be made with immediate effect to see that in the case of day-care centres, the remuneration of full time workers is not less than the wages earned by unskilled workers. However, the long-term goal should be to bring the trained full-time child care workers on par with primary school teachers. Part-time child care workers should be paid not less than minimum wages proportionate to their hours of work. To ensure proper supervision, ratio of supervisors to the number of ECCE centres should be improved. Considering the nature of work, which requires rapport with mothers and tenderness to children, ECCE workers and their supervisors should invariably be women.

7. Keeping in mind the role of ECCE as a support service in universalisation of elementary education, as well as for human resource development ECCE will be, in the first instance, directed to the most underprivileged groups, those who are still outside the mainstream of formal education. Some of these can be defined as follows:

i) very poor urban slum communities;

ii) ecologically deprived areas where children are required to fetch fuel, fodder, water and so other household chores;

iii) family labour and household chores in rural areas and artisan households;

iv) working children in the unorganised sector;

v) itinerant, or seasonal labour, who have a mobile transient life-style, like road workers;

vi) construction workers in urban and rural areas;

vii) landless agricultural labour;

viii) nomadic communities and pastoralists;

ix) forest dwellers and tribals in remote areas; and

x) residents of remote isolated hamlets.

Girls in these groups may require support services like child care, sometime in very small units. Special attention should be given to scheduled castes and scheduled tribes in all the above defined categories.

Targets and Phasing

8. Ethically speaking, every child should be assured access to the fulfilment of all basic needs. Yet, facing the existing realities of outreach and utilisation, it is suggested that 70 per cent of the target groups (children 0-6 years) should be covered by all services by 2000 AD, whereas health and nutrition services should be extended to all the needy groups as early as possible. By the end of the Seventh Plan, a modest network of ECCE facilities should be established in all tribal development blocks, blocks having substantial scheduled caste population and slums in large cities. A minimum of 2.50 lakh centres should be established by 1990. Though various schemes need

to be improved and expanded, this coverage will be predominantly achieved by expansion of ICDS. ECCE will be expanded to a level of 10 lakh centres by 1995 and 20 lakh by the year 20W. Most of the coverage will be through ICDS but diverse kinds of pre-primary education centres and day-care centres, mainly for the population group mentioned at para 6, will also be encouraged and supported.

9. The emphasis in short-term would be on upgradation, expansion and strengthening of the existing programmes. Efforts will also be made, to extend these programme to areas and target groups unserved by them so far. The programme of action in this behalf will consist of development of the following modular packages:

a) *Integrated Child Development Services*

Preschool education component needs to be strengthened in ICDS. For this following steps will be taken:

i) Each Anganwadi Workers' Training Centre should be given the responsibility of running at least 25 Anganwadi centres so as to provide the trainees with adequate field practice areas.

ii) The trainees should be placed for a minimum of one month in the Anganwadis for practical training.

iii) Instructional materials for use of trainers and the trainees should be developed.

iv) Materials for children—picture books, pictures, posters, minimum essential play materials—should be made available to all Anganwadis and replenished periodically.

v) The trainers, supervisors and CDPOs should be oriented through refresher courses in preschool education component and given field training so that it is strengthened both at pre-service and in-service levels.

vi) The CDPO's office should be developed into a Resource Centre.

A beginning will be made in ICDS by developing a small percentage of Anganwadis as day-care centres and effort will be made to coordinate the timings of ICDS Anganwadis with the primary schools.

b) *ECE Centres (Department of Education)*

The ECE scheme as it stands, does not have components of health and nutrition. Neither does it have any provision for the training of teachers. The following measures will, therefore, be taken with immediate effect:

i) Adding health and nutrition components;

ii) Provision for training the personnel;

iii) Supply of educational materials for children;

iv) Using play way method and discouraging teaching of 3R's; and

v) System of monitoring to be developed and linked with the renewal of grants.

c) *Balwadis Run by Voluntary Agencies*

There are varieties of patterns in the Balwadis. Each scheme has its own history and background. All programmes of child development implemented through voluntary agencies will have an integrated approach, offering a comprehensive package and avoiding duplication. Where this does not happen, the existing activities will be merged in some comprehensive and integrated programme. Most of the programmes run by voluntary agencies do not have all the components of health, nutrition and education. They need to be converted into total child development centres.

d) *Pre-Primary Schools of the State Governments and Municipalities*

They essentially focus on education. Therefore, they require:

i) Adding components of health and nutrition;

ii) Discouraging the early introduction of the 3R's;

iii) Using play-way method; and

iv) Developing a relationship between home and community.

e) *Day Care Centres*

The creches and day-care centres being run with CSWK support and otherwise need to be reviewed and strengthened on an immediate basis. The following requirements will be ensured:

i) Timing co-terminous with school working hours or mothers' working hours;

ii) Adequate, safe and hygienic space;

iii) Adequate child worker ratio;

iv) Drinking water;

v) Supplementary nutrition;

vi) Paramedical care under medical supervision;

vii) Minimum equipment including linen cradles;

viii) Toys and play materials; and

ix) Training and supervision of workers.

10. A further emphasis during Seventh and Eighth plan will be on experimentation for evolving low cost and

context-specific models. The models which are in experimentation stage at the moment would be encouraged and expanded. Appropriate agencies will undertake a survey of such models. Some of the models which are already being experimented and which have much promise are, as follows:

a) *Home-based model (from conception to 6 years):* This model involves developing techniques of stimulation that can be taught to and done by parents or other members of the family to foster child development. It requires: (i) training of local women who will play the leadership role in conducting home visits and encouraging family members to conduct stimulation programmes for their children, (ii) development of low cost play materials to be used by the family, (iii) development of audio and video programmes for the mass media for wide implementation, and (iv) creation of a mobile supervisory cadre.

b) *Day-care centres (from birth to 6 years):* This model is a support service to free older children and working women. Some voluntary organisations are successfully implementing these programmes. Such day-care centres should be established at all construction sites and other work centres where women are employed in substantial numbers. While support for voluntary agencies should be provided on a liberal scale by Government, the expenditure on the centres run on work sites should be the responsibility of the employers.

c) *Family day-care centre:* This is best suited for areas where the target group is very small and a day-care centre may or may not be viable. In this model, a suitable women from the same group is identified as the home care worker, and given the necessary materials, training, supervision, and infrastructural support, including food, to take care of five or six children in her own home. It is envisaged that every cluster of about 10 home-care units would be supervised, guided and supported by a supervisory worker who is competent to give the necessary support.

Training

11. In all models of ECCE programmes, the component of training will be strengthened. Training would include a strong component of field placement under supervision. As the early childhood care and education programmes are bound to expand considerably over the next two decades, corresponding training facilities will be made available for all levels of functionaries. Following would be some of the important parameters for meeting the training requirements:

   i) Initiating a two-year vocational course in ECCE at +2 level with the objective to create basic skills which can later be adopted through job training for specific situations;

   ii) Strengthening the educational content of ICDS functionaries, training by providing appropriate training inputs, resources, materials, etc., and extending it, where possible, to include a component of day care management;

   iii) Taking steps for setting up a higher course in ECCE for senior level functionaries of ICDS, trainers in the various training institutions and the supervisory personnel;

iv) Creating a system of a accreditation of training institutions dealing with ECCE and review of the existing training programmes; and

v) Working our appropriate, tasks specific, flexible models for day-care training at field level in rural areas.

12. Media support is essential for conveying to the parents and community the messages of ECCE. It is also necessary for the training of personnel in ECCE. Side-by-side with the development of meaningful programmes for the adults, attention should be paid to the development of stimulating programmes for children. Concerted efforts will be made by all concerned organisations such as Doordarshan, AIR, NCERT, NIPCCD and other related organisations in developing the software in all major regional languages.

Monitoring and Evaluation

13. The system of monitoring and evaluation will be strengthened on the following lines:

i) A Management Information System will be evolved for monitoring all ECCE programmes. Information will be collected, complied, analysed and acted upon at the block/local authority level. The flow of information to different levels (district, state, centre) will be so planned that control functions at these levels can be performed effectively without delay.

ii) Assistance will be sought from professional institutions and expert bodies for independent, objective evaluation that can identify gaps and problems and feasible alternatives for remedial action. All types of programmes should be got evaluated by independent agencies once in five years and the reports of the evaluations followed up in order to improve the quality of services.

iii) In order to assess the contributions of ECCE from time-to-time an Index of Human Development will be worked out which would include, among others, the following elements:

a) infant mortality rate;

b) incidence of malnutrition in the second year of life;

c) access to early stimulation and education; and

d) female literacy level.

Elementary Education, Non-Formal Education and Operation Blackboard

The Present Situation

1. Provision of free and compulsory education to all the children until they complete the age of 14 years is a Directive Principle of the Constitution. Determined efforts have made since independence towards the achievement of this goal. Between 1950-51 and 1984-85 the number of primary schools increased from approximately 2,10,000 to approximately 5,20,000 and the number of upper primary schools from 30,600 to 1,30,000. Even so, an acceptably large number of habitations are still without primary schools and nearly one-third of the schools in rural areas have only one teacher. The emphasis so far has been on enrolment of children—approximately 95 per cent children in 6-11 age-group and 50 per cent children in 11-14 age-group are enrolled in schools, the corresponding figure for girls being 77 per cent and 36 per cent respectively. However, nearly 60 per cent children drop out between Classes I-V and 75

per cent between Classes I-VIII. In urban areas there is overcrowding in schools and the condition of buildings, furniture facilities and equipment is unsatisfactory in almost all parts of the, country. Rapid expansion, which was not accompanied by sufficient investment of resources, has caused a deterioration in academic standards. A programme of non-formal education has been started but in terms of spread and quality it is rather unsatisfactory.

The Policy and Targets

2. NPE gives an unqualified priority to universalisation elementary education (UEE). The thrust in elementary education emphasises: (i) universal enrolment and universal retention of children upto 14 years of age, and (ii) a substantial improvement in the quality of education.

3. The child-centred approach commanded in NPE attempts to build the academic programme and school activities around the child. The policy also recognises that unattractive school environment, unsatisfactory condition of buildings and insufficiency of instructional material function as demotivating factors for children and their parents. The policy, therefore, calls for a drive for a substantial improvement of primary schools and provision of support services. A variety of measures have been proposed for securing participation of girls and of children from the Scheduled Castes and Scheduled Tribes families, other educationally backward sections and minorities.

4. Conclusive data is not available regarding the number of working children. However, it has been assumed in the policy that a large number of

out-of-school children are unable to avail themselves of the benefits of schooling because they have to work to supplement family income or otherwise assist the family. NPE proposes taking up of a large and systematic programme of non-formal education, for these children and for children of habitations without schools. The emphasis in NPE is on organisation of flexible programmes which are relevant to the needs of the learners and the quality of which is comparable with the corresponding stages of formal education.

5. The measures proposed to improvement in quality of elementary education include reform of the content and process of education, improvement in school building and other facilities, provision of additional teachers and the comprehensive programme of teacher education. Minimum levels of learning are to be laid down for each stage, which would naturally include laying down such norms for the primary and upper primary stages.

6. In addition to UEE, NPE also envisages a common school structure throughout the country. Acknowledging that the 10+2+3 structure has now been accepted in all parts of the country, a suggestion has been made that the primary stage should consist of 5 years, followed by 3 years of upper primary.

7. In the past, the targets set for UEE have not corresponded to the investment required for achievement of the goal, nor has it been possible to create the mobilisation which is essential for this purpose. Taking a more practical view of the matter, NPE limits itself to proposing that all children by the time they attain the age of about 11 years will have five years of schooling, or its equivalent through the

non-formal stream, and likewise it will be ensured that free and compulsory education upto 14 years of ages is provided to all children by 1995.

Implementation Strategies

8. The central feature of the implementation strategy will be area-specific and population-specific planning. About 75 per cent of the out-of-school children are in nine States: Andhra Pradesh, Assam, Bihar, Jammu & Kashmir, Madhya Pradesh, Orissa, Rajasthan, Uttar Pradesh, and West Bengal. While these States have been treated as educationally backward, enough attention has not been paid in the past to educationally backward packets and groups in other States. Even within the educationally backward states there are wide disparities which require special treatment. Sustained efforts will be made to revitalise the educational system of the backward states and effort will also be made to see that all backward areas and population pockets make progress to keep in step with others in their millieu. The other elements of strategy will consists of the following:

   a) Children of all families in the country will be provided access to elementary education of good quality.

   b) In view of the role of education in removal of disparities, special measures will be taken to ensure that whatever the socio-economic background of the children, they get opportunity to achieve success of a level which approximates to the level of children from comparatively better-off sections of society, and the country moves apace in the direction of the Common School System as spelt out in the 1968 policy.

c) A nation-wide programme of school improvement, with required multi-level and multi-dimensional planning, will be launched to alter the present situation of institutional stagnation and social apathy. Reference has been made elsewhere about reform of the teacher education system for improvement of the quality of education.

d) The country's faith and its future generations will be exemplified in the system of elementary education, which will get geared around the centrality of the child.

e) For their healthy development and to ensure that they enjoy conditions of freedom and dignity, the education system will strive to have all children in whole-time schools of good quality, and till that becomes possible they will be provided opportunities of part-time non-formal education.

f) Since NPE lays down that children who complete a stage of education would have achieved certain prescribed skills and competencies, the emphasis will now shift from sheer enrolment to retention and quality of education.

g) Keeping in view the fact that the situation regarding elementary education varies from one part of the country to another, and sometimes within one district, and even one block, the process of planning will be decentralised and the teachers as well as the local community fully involved in this process.

Mobilisation for UEE—A Prerequisite or success

9. An analysis of the achievements and failures in UEE

shows that we have tended to excessively rely on opening of schools, appointment of teachers and launching of enrolment drives. The above mentioned strategies will make a qualitative change in the implementation of the UEE programme in the coming years. These strategies will, however, succeed only if a genuine mobilisation based on participatory involvement of teachers and the community, can be ensured. In specific terms, the prerequisites for the proposed programme of UEE are as follows:

1) UEE can come about only as a result of an upsurge—involving all the people concerned. The political parties, particularly their local level constructive workers' will.

2) Involvement of teachers at all stages of planning and implementation of the new strategy will be ensured. This will take the form of systematic consultations with their unions and associations, ensuring that they are fully involved in micro-level planning for UEE.

3) As indicated in the section on management of Education, the local community will be involved in all aspects of UEE. For all practical purposes, the primary schools and non-formal education centres will be accountable to it. Due care will be taken to ensure that women, youth, and the sections of society who have remained deprived of educational opportunities have and effective voice.

4) All agencies and individuals who have carried the confidence of the community and who can make a positive contribution to UEE will be involved. These would include youth clubs, *Mahila Mandals*, voluntary agencies and social activist groups, as well as local development workers, retired teachers, ex-servicemen, etc.

5) Making the system work is of the greatest importance. Hardly any change can take place unless the schools and NFE centres are properly run, teachers/instructors provide instruction and other processes of education are followed.

Universal Provision or Facilities

10. The Fourth All India Educational Survey (1978-79) revealed that 1,90,000 habitations were without schooling facilities. Since then several new schools have been opened, but habitations have also come into existence. Considering the whole situation it would be correct to say that the number of habitations without school is still very large and that many of them are likely to be fairly large habitations. All state governments will ensure that all habitations with a population of 300 (200 in the case of tribal, hilly and desert areas) will be provided a primary school within the 7th Plan. Effort will also be made, on the lines of Mobile Creches, to set up special schools for specific duration for building and construction workers and other categories of people who shift their residence.

11. Detailed school mapping exercises will be initiated forth-with, and completed by the end of 1987-88, in order to prepare a master plan of universal provision of facilities for EE. NIEPA has already initiated some exercise in this regard. The basis of' school mapping would be to ensure that every habitation which can potentially have 50 children in the primary school should be provided one and an tipper primary school opened on primary school catchment basis. For persons belonging to SC/ST and other deprived sections, residential schools and hostels will be provided on a much larger scale. The programme of

Ashram Schools will also be improved and enlarged. Effort will be made towards creation of an inexpensive system of hostels, using the school building and providing a kitchen room, where local villagers would be engaged on part-time basis to assist with cooking and supervision. Possibility of providing free foodgrains to the students in those hostels out of the accumulated stocks in the country will be explored.

Enrolment and Retention

12. According to the Expert Committee on population projections, set up by the Planning Commission, the estimated population in 6-11 age-group in 1989-90 will be about 9.61 crores. The present population estimate for this age-group can be taken to be 9.00 crores. Against this the enrolment figures for 1984-85 are 8.54 crores, the gross enrolment ratio for boys and girls being 110 and 74 per cent. However, nearly 22 per cent of the enrolled are outside 6-11 age-group, mostly over-age. The first aspect of the new programme of universalisation is that for some years to come we should have no objection so along as children complete 5 years of education, or its equivalent through the non-formal stream, by the time they complete about 14 years of age.

13. Enrolment by itself is of little importance if children do not continue education beyond even one year, many of them not seeing the school for more than a few days. Emphasis will, therefore, now shift from enrolment to retention and completion by all children of at least 5 years of education. Enrolment drives will be replaced by systematic house-to-house survey in which the teachers, in cooperation with the village community, will discuss with the parents the relevance of' schooling and regularity of attendance.

Children for whom it is just not possible to participate in whole-day schools, will be enrolled in the non-formal education centres, but it will be ensured that every child in every family receives instruction. It is also important that all children regularly attend school or non-formal education centres. In the event of a child not coming for 2-3 days at a stretch the teacher and/or members of the Village Education Committee will approach the family of the child and persuade them to make the child resume regular attendance. This family-wise and child-wise design of action to ensure that every child regularly attends school or non-formal education centre, continues his/her education at a pace suitable to him/her, and complete at least five years of schooling, or its equivalent at the non-formal education centre, is what is intended by micro-planning at para 5.12 of NPE.

14. By making elementary education child-centred, we would be introducing a long-awaited reform in the system. The most important aspect of this reform will be to make education a joyful, inventive and satisfying learning activity, rather than a system of role and cheerless, authoritarian instruction. Much of it would depend on reform of the curriculum and co-curricular activities, in respect of which mention has been made in another section. Considering that children in rural primary schools are subjected to all kinds of manual tasks, it needs to be clarified that while manual work by children is not to be shunned it should be an educational activity rather than irksome draft. Practically all states have already banned corporal punishment. But it is still widely prevalent. Through programmes of teachers' education and strict supervision this practice will be effectively prevented. Each District Board of

Education will have the power to determine the days of vacation and they would be asked to relate them to agricultural seasons, ensuring at the same time that the number of instructional days does not fall below 220. The non-detention policy has also been accepted in principle for quite some time. In practice, however, for one reason or other, a large percentage of children still repeat their classes. Non-detention policy will be effectively implemented upto Class VIII, while also ensuring that the minimum learning competencies are reached. For this purpose various measures referred to the section on Examination Reform, will be taken.

15. A comprehensive system of incentives and support services will be provided for girls and children of the economically weaker sections of society. A reference to these has been made in the sections on the Scheduled Castes, Scheduled Tribes, Minorities, Education for Women's Equality, etc. The following items have special relevance to the new strategy of emphasis on retention:

    a) Establishment of day-care centres for pre-school children and infants—as part of strengthening of ICDS, provision of adequate support to the ongoing programmes, and by establishment of a network of new centres;

    b) Provision to the girls of all families below the poverty line two sets of free uniforms, free textbooks and stationery, and attendance incentives; and

    c) Free transportation in state roadways buses to children attending elementary schools.

1 *National Policy on Education (NPE):* Programme of Action. A comprehensive system of rewards and recognition will be created for individuals and

institutions who contribute in a significant manner retention of children in primary schools/NFE centres. These rewards may be given to the villages, schools/NFE centres, and to the teachers/instructors concerned. The amount of reward will be enough to ensure that it serves as motivation.

Enrolment in 11-14 Age-Group

17. Keeping in view the high transition rate from primary to upper primary stage, enrolment in the 11-14 age-group will automatically increase after universalisation of primary education. This would be further strengthened as a result of universal provision of upper primary school facilities in the Eighth Plan, and by creation of mechanisms for testing the children of non-formal stream for lateral entry into the formal system. These measures will be supplemented by a system of compulsory education legislation. The States which have not enacted such law would be advised modified on the following lines:

   a) Requiring employers of working children to provide rest and nutrition as well as arrangements for part time education of good quality, with provision for exemplary punitive action against employers who fail to do so;

   b) Involving the local community and the parents in implementation of UEE and in ensuring that educational facilities are provided to their satisfaction;

   c) Establishing schools and/or non-formal education centres of satisfactory quality within an easy reach of all children; and

   d) Creating necessary machinery for impleme-ntation of the acts, emphasising the facilitating aspects rather than the punitive ones.

Common Structure

18. In the meetings of the CABE and NDC in May, 1986, a consensus has already been reached in regard to the need for switching over to a common structure for the first ten year of schooling.

19. The States where the first ten years are divided into four years of primary, three years of tipper primary and three years of high school, will attempt to switch over to 5+3+2 pattern by 1995 so that it coincides with the target year for UEE. These states would need to build additional classrooms in primary schools and more teachers will also be needed. However, this would be partially set off by the savings of space and staff in high schools. It will be necessary for these states/UTs to do a detailed exercise to assess the requirement of classrooms, teachers, and funds. Similarly, syllabi, textual materials and school facilities would have to be readjusted and the examination system would have to be reorganised.

Operation Blackboard (OB)

20. The purpose of OB is to ensure provision of minimum essential facilities in primary schools—material facilities as well as learning equipment. Use of the word 'operation' implies that there is an urgency in this programme, that goals are clear and well-defined, and that government and the people are determined to achieve those goals within a predetermined timeframe.

21. OB envisages: (i) two reasonably large rooms that are usable in all weather; (ii) necessary toys and games material; (iii) blackboards; (iv) maps; (v) charts; and other learning materials. The specific items to be provided in each school under OB is given in the

Annex. In regard to the buildings to be constructed the following points need to be mentioned:

- — Construction of essential buildings for primary schools will be the first charge on NREP and RLEGP funds. Those resources will be supplemented by other appropriate schemes.
- — Village Education Committees will be required to give undertaking for maintenance and upkeep of buildings and other structures.
- — Primary school-wise inventories of available structures will be prepared for systematic planning.
- — Inexpensive building designs will be prepared keeping in view the agro-climatic conditions and utilising locally available materials.
- — Steps will be taken for obtaining land for playgrounds.

22. It is proposed to take the CD block/municipal area as the unit and to prepare a project for it on the basis of survey of these facilities in each school in that block/municipal area. Although the Fifth Educational Survey is soon being taken up by the NCERT, its data will not become available for some months, and compilation and analysis will take still longer. To cover at least 10 per cent blocks and urban schools in the same proportion under the programme in 1986-87 and 20 per cent in 1987-88 it is proposed to conduct a quick survey in a specifically designed simple format in these blocks/ municipal area by 30th September 1986 so that the data can be complied and project reports prepared by 30.11.1986 and approval accorded by 31.12.1986. Empowered Committees will be set up at the district level to consider and approve the block/municipal

area projects. The funds for Operation Blackboard would be provided by the Government of India to the State Governments on advance/reimbursement basis. The results of Fifth Educational Survey would form the basis for block/municipal area projects for the remaining 30 per cent blocks/municipal area in 1988-89 and 40 per cent blocks/municipal area in 1989-90.

23. Procedures for procurement, supply and use of equipment envisaged under OB will have to be evolved keeping in view the special needs of primary schools and also ensuring that the costs are kept low. For this purpose specific norms will be laid down. The first thing will be to specify the various items so as to ensure quality. This work will be done by NCERT, in association with state agencies. Particular attention will be paid to procurement procedures because the general system of purchase by tenders tends to lead to purchase of sub-standard materials. The capacity available in polytechnics, ITIS, secondary and higher secondary schools will be geared to produce the materials required by the school system, particularly under OB. Since unimaginative and rigid provisions of audit and supervision have deterred teachers in many places from using teaching aids at all, amendment of accounting procedures will also require to be worked out. Lastly, the teachers will have to be oriented and encouraged to use this material in day-to-day teaching. The mass training of teachers in the summer of 1987 and 1988 will include this aspect. This will be reinforced by supervision by District Boards of Education and DIETs.

24. There is a very large number of single teacher schools in the rural areas. It is obvious that a programme of quality improvement must include

provision of at least one more teacher in these schools. This will be attempted during the Seventh Plan and a detailed programme prepared for providing one teacher per class during the Eighth Plan. Every effort will be made to ensure that one of the two teachers in every school is a woman, and for this purpose, depending on circumstances obtaining in different areas, local educated women may be selected, provided special training and opportunities for improving their qualifications. Such a strategy may also become necessary for male teachers in remote rural areas.

The New Programme or Non-formal Education

25. This programme assumes that NFE can result in provision of education comparable in quality with formal schooling. Modern technological tools—such as solar packs for provision of power in NFE centres, audio-visual aids, radio-cassette player-will be used to improve the learning environment of NFE centres, and learning material of high quality will be developed taking into account the fact that children who work have several assets on which their education should be built. The essential characteristics of NFE are organisational flexibility, relevance of curriculum, diversity in learning activities to relate them to the learners' needs, and decentralisation of management. Efforts will be made to evolve different models of non-formal education programmes and agencies implementing the programme will be encouraged to evolve and adopt the most suitable model depending upon the requirement of targets groups.

26. *Special features of NFE*: In addition to these characteristics, NFE will have certain features which will help in maintenance of quality of the programme. These features include:

a) a learner-centred approach with the instructor as a facilitator;

b) emphasis on learning rather than teaching, and for this purpose the capability of the children to learn from each other would be highlighted;

c) organisation of activities so as to enable learners to progress at their own pace;

d) use of efficient techniques to ensure fast pace of learning and provision of proper lighting arrangements at the NFE centres and necessary equipment;

e) stress on continuous learner evaluation and establishment of evaluation centres for evaluation and certification of learners;

f) in terms of scholastic achievements (particularly language and maths), following the norms set in the formal system, both because of its desirability *per se* and because it is essential for entry into the formal structures;

g) creation of participatory learning environment and treating the children with the regard they deserve as persons engaged in productive activities;

h) organisation of joyful extra-curricular activities including singing and dancing, plays and skits, games and sports, excursions, etc.;

i) ensuring that all facilities and incentives given to girls, children of SC/ST, and others in the formal system, are made available in the non-formal system as well, in addition to provision of free textbooks and stationery to all pupils.

27. *Instructors and their training*: The instructor is the most important factor in the implementation of NFE.

The criteria for the selection of the instructor would include:

- being local,
- being already motivated,
- acceptable to the community, and
- preferably from the weaker sections of society, should have given some evidence of work in the community.

28. Keeping in view the importance of enrolment of girls, and also the fact that NFE has the potentiality of developing into a major programme of women's development, wherever possible women will be appointed as instructors.

29. Training of non-formal education personnel, particularly the instructors, is the key to the success of the programme. Initial training as well as recurrent training are both crucial. By and large, training days for the instructors would be about 30 days in the first year and about 20 days in the subsequent years. The need for participatory training, based on the experiences of the participants, is now well-recognised. Actualisation of such training will call for considerable planning and investment. A variety of agencies will be involved and help taken of diverse training aids and educational technology, including TV and VCR.

30. *Supervision administration*: In the administrative restructuring, the most important place belongs to the supervisor, on whom depends to a great extent the quality of the programme. The work of supervision may be entrusted to whole-time NFE supervisors with about 20-25 centres under her/his charge, or preferably to trained local youth.

31. Approximately 100 NFE centres will comprise a project, which would be taken up in a compact and contiguous area coterminous, as for as possible, with a CD Block. The main functions at the project level would be: (i) to select the supervisors, (ii) to generally supervise the programme, (iii) to promote interagency linkages to give development orientation to the field programme, (iv) to monitor the programme, (v) to ensure provision of materials and supplies, etc. Strengthening is also envisaged at the district and state levels. Wherever possible the administrative and supervisory structure for NFE and adult education will be amalgamated—including the programmes to be taken up through panchayati raj bodies and voluntary agencies.

32. *Involvement of voluntary agencies and panchayati raj institutions*: Several voluntary agencies have, in the past successfully organised NFE programmes. Very often voluntary agencies have bands of committed workers who have the capability to establish rapport with the local community and they can also function with flexibility and dynamism. Several panchayati raj institutions have also shown keen interest in NFE and they have the capability to run such programmes. It is proposed to take positive measures to involve in NFE as many voluntary agencies and panchayati raj institutions as possible, which can suitably take up this programme. It is also proposed to improve the existing administrative arrangements for support to VAs. Proposals will be examined by a grant-in-aid committee and where necessary a representative of the voluntary agency would be invited for discussion with the committee. Projects of voluntary agencies will be entertained for a period of 3-4 years. They would be required to send the initial proposals through the State

Government but at the subsequent stages the voluntary agencies will directly approach the Ministry for release of grants-in-aid. The State Governments would, of course, be expected to oversee the implementation of voluntary agencies' projects.

33. *Continuing education*: Scope for continuing their education is important for all learners. The strength of the PNFE will depend to a considerable extent on our being able to link the initial programmes of NFE with effective programmes of continuing education. This has several implications for PNFE. (a) Arrangements will be made for testing of children in NFE stream with reference to an equivalent stage in the formal system and specific instructions issued to facilitate lateral entry into the formal system for students of non-formal education stream. (b) Non-formal education centres would insist on children completing education at least V Class level, and arrangements of non-formal education unto Class VIII would be provided wherever necessary. Effort would also be made to link non-formal courses with the Open Schools. (c) Scholarships to the needy children, particularly working children, will be provided to enable them to continue education in the formal system. (d) NFE programme would also be linked with the schemes of public libraries, Jana Shikshan Nilayams, etc. (c) Vocational and technical courses of a wide variety would be provided for children and youth who come out of the non-formal stream.

34. *Financial pattern and flexibility regarding application*: It is proposed that in the Seventh Plan, as in the Sixth Plan, there will be the following components of the non-formal education programme, to be applied in the 9 educationally backward state:

a) Assistance to State Government for setting up and running non-formal centres (boys and girls both) on 50:50 basis;

b) Assistance to State Governments for setting up and running non-formal education centres exclusively for girls on 90:10 basis;

c) Assistance to voluntary agencies for setting up and running non-formal education centres on 100 per cent basis;

d) Assistance to academic institutions for taking up innovative projects and research and evaluation activities in the field of non-formal education on 100 per cent basis.

Even in the educationally advanced States there are several regions and client-groups which call for special support. These include:

— the hilly tracts,

— predominantly tribal areas known for educational backwardness,

— urban slums, and

— projects for education of working children, etc.

It is proposed to extend these schemes to these areas also. Extension of schemes to other regions and client-groups may also be considered.

Evaluation and Monitoring

35. The present system of evaluation and monitoring will not suffice for the new strategies of UEE. In the new evaluation and monitoring system the main features will be as follows:

a) A critical point of evaluation in the educational system is the progress of the learners. Hence, as mentioned elsewhere in this section as well as in the section on examination reform, the greatest attention will be paid to creating a scientific system of evaluation of learners, which would serve both as the basis for improvement of the academic programme and as the measures of the overall quality of elementary education system.

b) Since the principal accountability of the primary/tipper primary school system and NFE programmes is to the local community, the latter will also be mainly responsible for monitoring these programmes and for taking necessary corrective steps.

c) Just as the teacher/NFE instructors are to be involved in the planning and implementing of UEE, they will also be involved in concurrent, participatory evaluation.

d) The emphasis in the monitoring system will shift from collection of information on enrolment to retention of children, regularity of attendance and levels of achievement. All instrumentalities of MIS will be changed accordingly.

e) The main responsibility for implementation of OB will rest with the District Board of Education, likewise the monitoring and evaluation responsibility would also rest with it. In doing so DBE will take the assistance of DIET.

f) The evaluation would be built into the NFE programme as an integral part and the instructors and supervisors will undertake these exercises on a continuing basis. The basic unit for collection of MIS data in NFE programme will be the project.

g) The State Advisory Boards of Education and CABE will set up separate committees to review the progress of UEE. For this purpose they will be assisted by NIEPA, NCERT, SCERT and other suitable national and State level agencies of education and of social science research.

Annexure. Essential Facilities At The Primary Stage

1. Teacher's equipment:
   a) Syllabus,
   b) Textbooks,
   c) Teacher's guides.
2. Classroom teaching materials:
   a) Maps: district, state, country,
   b) Plastic globes,
   c) Educational charts.
3. Play materials and toys:
   a) Wisdom blocks,
   b) Surface tension,
   c) Bird and animal puzzle,
   d) Animal world,
   e) Balance and weights,
   f) Magnifying glasses,
   g) Magnets,
   h) Measuring tape,
   i) Cleanliness, nutrition, language and number charts.
4. Games equipment:
   a) Skipping rope.
   b) Balls: football, volleyball, rubber balls,

   c) Air pump,
   d) Ring,
   e) Swing rope with tyre.
5. Primary science kit
6. Mini tool kit
7. Two-in-one audio equipment
8. Books for library:
   a) Reference books: dictionaries and encyclopaedia,
   b) Children's books (at least 200),
   c) Magazine, journals and newspapers for teachers and children.
9. School bell
10. Musical instruments
    a) Dholak or Tabla,
    b) Harmonium,
    c) Manjira.
11. Contingency money with teacher
12. All weather classrooms
    a) Classrooms,
    b) Toilets-one for boys and one for girls,
    c) Mats and furniture for students and teachers.
13. Black board
14. Chalk and duster
15. Water facility
16. Trash can

Secondary Education and Navodaya Vidyalayas

Present Situation

There were 56323 secondary/higher secondary schools

and 1,23,000 upper primary schools in 1983. This would give a ratio of 1:2.5. The enrolment at secondary level was 97,45,519 and at higher secondary level 51,01,435 in 1983. There are unserved areas in the country where there is no school for 10 to 20 kms like in some tribal areas, desert or hilly areas where the low density of population does not allow enough children to be enrolled. An area also be unserved through near a school if a physical barrier like river or mountain separates it.

Prerequisites and Broad Parameters of Strategy Envisaged

Secondary and higher secondary education is on the one hand terminal for those who enter the world of work after this stage. For such people a strengthened vocational scheme should form the main plank of strategy. For the rest it is preparatory to higher education and, therefore, a good grounding in the subject area should be provided along with learning orientation. The improvement in management system of which perhaps the school complex system and improved supervisory system are the most important should be the main programmes during the Seventh Plan and would continue thereafter. A flexible and interactive teaching programme supported by adequate laboratories and libraries would be a pre-requisite for learning-oriented education. A programme of curricular reform and examination/ evaluation reform would provide conditions for a good grounding in subject areas.

The policy relating to secondary education implies extension of the school system in the unserved areas consolidating the existing facilities and providing special arrangements for the gifted children and the high achievers. This would mean that it would require:

a) programme to ensure access to secondary education being widened to cover unserved areas;
b) programme of consolidation in other areas/schools, and
c) programme of setting up Navodaya Vidyalayas.

Programmes and Implementation

As a short-term measure the State Governments would be persuaded to open secondary schools in unserved areas taking blocks as a unit having a lover ratio than 1:2.5 duly considering the present distance of habitation from the nearest secondary school and population in the unserved habitations. As a medium and long term measure a programme of school mapping in each state for locating schools to cover all areas will be taken up. The technique of school mapping will be followed both for planning and implementation for location of secondary schools on the basis of clearly defined norms and standards. Special emphasis will be laid in this study on backward areas, areas predominantly inhabitated by SC/ST and schooling facilities for girls. School clusters will be established with secondary school as its lead school and upper primary schools in the catchment area. The ratio of upper primary to primary schools will be at 1.3 as recommended by the Kothari Commission. This programme would be taken up by NIEPA in cooperation with SCERTs. This exercise can be completed by 1988 and from 1989 onwards it could be implemented. By 2000 the unserved areas will be fully served. The funds required for this purpose which cannot be estimated now will be fully met by the State Government only.

3. For the products of non-formal education at elementary stage many of whom will continue to find difficult to attend full time school and for the

working people who have missed the secondary school and other of this type, a flexible, non-formal arrangement is needed at secondary and higher secondary level.

This requirement is proposed to be met by open schools. Open schools would be established in a phased manner by 1990 with a resource centre in each district. These resource centres should be located in or linked to the selected secondary teacher training institutions or the district institutes of education.

4. It is known that the secondary and higher secondary schools are under-provided particularly in the rural areas in terms of buildings, teachers and school facilities but the extent of these shortages have not been surveyed in all aspects. The programme of consolidation envisaged in the policy will have the following components of which the cost cannot be precisely estimated:

a) Adequate playground facilities where needed will have to be provided by making available nearby vacant land and in other places by arranging for sharing of such facility with neighbouring school as a priority programme during the Seventh Plan.

b) A programme for construction of additional classrooms and laboratory facilities in schools to the extent they are deficient will be taken up. School education is mainly looked after by the State Government and local bodies. If possible the Central Government may consider supplementation of resources.

c) Every school must have laboratories and other facilities as specified in the terms of recognition of the Board of Secondary/Higher Secondary Education to which it is affiliated. These norms have been developed by the NCERT and KVS also. Taking into consideration the past experience that equipment once given is not replaced and even maintained it is suggested that community participation by way of student contribution at the rate of Rs. 10 to 15 per month should be levied, except from girls and other exempt from payment of tuition fee. This collection should remain in the school for replacement and maintenance purposes.

d) The teacher competencies would be improved by attracting better qualified people to the profession as envisaged in the policy and by improving the pre-service and in-service training programmes through strengthened secondary teacher training institutions. The process will begin straightaway and will be continued for consistently upgrading teachers' competencies.

e) As envisaged in the policy, the core-curriculum will play an important role in educational consolidation. This will be followed by overall improvement in curriculum, the textual material, teaching practices and examination/evaluation methods.

f) The Kothari Commission suggested that the ratio of higher secondary and secondary schools should be 1:3. This should be ensured. A large number of higher secondary schools have only one or two streams out of humanities, science and commerce and most do not have vocational stream. As an important programme in the process of consolidation, schools should be helped to have all the three streams and a vocational stream in selected schools. This will be the responsibility of the State Government concerned. Vocational stream would be set up with the assistance of the Government of India as may be determined.

5. The programme for bright children has two parts: one is for potentially high achievers particularly in the areas who are substantially left uncovered by the present system and the other is the programme for the gifted students who can be expected to make original contribution in their subject areas if properly nurtured.

   Under the scheme of Navodaya Vidyalayas for catering to the category of high achievers one such Vidyalaya will be set up in each district during the Seventh Five Year Plan period. These schools will make available good quality education irrespective of the parent's capacity to pay and their socio-economic background. In these schools there will be 75 per cent reservation for children from rural areas. There will be reservation for SC and ST as per their actual Population in the district subject to a minimum of nationally prescribed figure of 15 and 7th for SC & ST respectively. An effort will be made to cover girls to the extend of 1/3 in a school. Education will be free including boarding and lodging in these schools. These schools will be affiliated to the Central Board of Secondary Education.

   The gifted students frequently have pronounced competence in a limited subject area accompanied by indifference in certain other areas. Therefore, arrangements for such students cannot be fitted into regular courses of study. Special arrangements for such students will have to provide teaching/learning on modular basis for every small group of students in a small number of subjects of interest to them. Such arrangements will be characterised by large facilities, higher teacher-student ratio and regular participation by professionals in leaching programmes. A detailed project for this purpose should be worked out by a specially constituted group within one year. Arrangements will be designed for implementation within the present system for such students.

Vocationalisation of Education

Present Position

1. In 1976, the National Council of Educational Research and Training (NCERT) document 'Higher Secondary Education and its Vocationalisation' was presented to the country setting out a model conceptual framework for implementation. The programme for vocationalisation of higher secondary education was initiated in 1976. Since then it has been implemented in 10 States and 5 Union Territories. A number of other States are likely to introduce vocationalisation in the academic year 1986-87. The current intake in the vocational stream is of the order of 72,000. Only about 2.5 per cent of students population entering higher secondary stage is covered by vocationalisation so far.
2. Being aware of the importance and need for diversification of secondary education—its vocationalisation, the Ministry of Human Resource Development, Government of India and NCERT have initiated many actions and made many proposals. Evaluation studies of vocational programmes in most of the States were conducted to provide the findings to the States for improving implementation.
3. Inspite of all these efforts, the scheme of vocationalisation of education has not yet picked up. There have been many factors responsible for the slow progress, such as, absence of a well coordinated management system, unemployability of vocational pass outs, mis-match between demand and supply,

reluctance in accepting the concept by the society, absence of proper provisions for professional growth and career advancement for the vocational pass outs etc. Renewed efforts are being made in many States to accelerate progress. Urgent steps to strengthen the vocational education system are therefore imperative.

Management of Vocational Education

4. While the factors contributing to the rather unsatisfactory progress on the vocationalisation front may be many, the single most important aspect is the inadequate organisational structure to the task and its consequent inability to implement the accepted policies.

5. At present the management systems for various sectors of vocational education work in isolation and with hardly any coordination either at the national, regional or state level.

6. At national level, the post-secondary vocational education (vocationalisation) and vocational education for the out-of-school population are being looked after by many organisations under different ministries (like agriculture, health, rural development, human resource development, etc.) without having proper coordination and linkages. Vocational programmes cover a wide range of disciplines. These include agriculture, business and commerce, engineering, and technology, health and paramedical services, home science, humanities and others.

7. At state level the system is still fragmented and inadequate. A few states have a full time directorate, the others have a middle level official looking after the vocationalisation programme in addition to his

other responsibilities. No mechanism is available to coordinate the vocational programme at district levels and to undertake activities like, district level need surveys for identification of manpower requirements, for developing need-based vocational courses, etc. In addition, provision made for activities like curriculum design, resource material preparation, training of vocational teachers etc. are inadequate considering the massive nature of the task.

8. Keeping in view the variety of functions to be performed in planning and implementing programmes of vocational education and the scale of operations commensurate with the desired changes at post-primary, post-secondary and post-higher secondary stages, it is necessary to organise an effective management system.

Vocational Education Programmes: Work Experience in General Education

9. At the primary state of education from Classes I to 5 Socially Useful Productive Work (SUPW)/Work Experience (WE) forms an integral part of the curriculum in many states. Inspite of its good intentions of developing proper attitudes, and actual implementation both in coverage and quality leaves much to be desired.

10. At the middle school stage SUPW/WE programmes aim at developing confidence and sufficient psychomotor skills to students to enter the world of work directly or through certain occupational training courses.

Secondary Stage (Classes 9-10)

11. The SUPW/WE programmes for the secondary stage

are viewed as a linear extension of that for the middle stage. These activities at secondary stage are also expected to enable students to opt for vocational programmes at the +2 level with better appreciation and undertaking. It may also be mentioned that a significant number of students drop out after this stage. Hence, the programmes of SUPW/WE are expected to ensure to modest preparation for students before they leave the school to enable them to choose an occupation. Such pre-vocational courses are to be handled by teachers with specific skills and competence. These programmes also need proper resources within the school.

Higher Secondary Stage

12. The vocational courses at higher secondary stage are to be regarded not as a preparation for the college, but as a period for preparing an increasingly large number of school-leavers for different vocations in life. The need for vocationalisation of higher secondary education has been conceded by all, but the problems in its implementation may be appreciated by the fact that only a small percentage of students population has been covered by vocationalisation in the past nine years (1976-85). The estimated number of students seeking admission to +2 in 1985 is of the order of 25 lakhs. Even if 10 per cent of this population was to be diverted for vocational courses, the number should have over 2.50 lakhs, against the present intake of 0.72 lakhs. The problem call be further appreciated, if this data is seen against the Kothari Commission's recommendation, expecting a diversion of 50 per cent of 10+ students for vocational education.

Vocational Education: Other Formal Programmes

13. The country has developed over the years, a network

of vocational schools, vocational institutes and polytechnics. Nearly 2 per cent to 3 per cent of the school going children enter such institutes-like Industrial Training Institutes (ITIs), Junior Technical Schools etc.

These institutions handle essentially full time students who meet the need of organised sector. The annual intake is of the order of 5 lakhs.

14. Kothari Commission has visualised that at 8+ about 20 per cent of the students will step off the general stream and enter schools of vocational education. Similarly, a large percentage of 10+ students are to be diverted to such vocational institutions. However, the present vocational institutions are not able to cater to this large number of students after 8+ and 10+ There is, therefore, a need for expansion of the regular vocational education programmes-in terms opening more institutions and introduction of new vocational areas.

Vocational Education at Tertiary Level

15. One of the factors responsible for the slow progress of vocationalisation of secondary education is lack of opportunities for the vocational pass-outs for their progressional growth and career advancement.
16. The current prejudice against vocational education will not disappear unless a reasonable chance of worthwhile employment or an advantage in moving upwards into a professional or general programme of education is provided to the students of vocational courses at the secondary level.
17. Such programmes could include diploma, special degree courses, general degree courses, professional degree courses. At present, opportunities for further education for students of vocational stream in +2 are

almost non-existent. Hence suitable strategies are to be evolved for providing opportunities for the vocational products to enter appropriate 'tertiary level' programmes.

Apprenticeship Training

18. The products of the vocational stream at +2 level are quite distinct form those from the ITIs and polytechnics who have been covered under the Craftsmen and Technician Apprenticeship Training Schemes. It has been strongly recommended by several committees connected with vocational education that vocational students of the +2 stage should be brought wider the umbrella of apprentice scheme as in important catalyst for the promotion of vocational education. At present, a few of the 120 vocational courses offered at the +2 level in the country are selected for the special vocationalised education training scheme launched by MHRD. Appropriate actions are to be taken for introducing apprentice scheme to as many vocational courses as required.

Other Vocational Programmes

19. The vocational courses in Higher Secondary Schools and Vocational and Technical Training Schools/ Institutes cater only to the requirements of organised sector of the economy. However, it is the unorganised sector which absorbs the bulk of workforce. Consequently one sees the phenomenon of mounting unemployment among the educated at one end and shortage of plumbers, car mechanics, electricians, carpenters and manpower in numerous other trades at the other end.

20. It is estimated that about 80 per cent of the student population do not go beyond Class X. The dropouts upto and inclusive of class 8 are over 120 lakhs per year. Roughly 20 lakh of boys and girls cross Class VIII but do not go beyond Class X. All of them form a large pool of unskilled labour force. They need opportunities for training in some skills either in their traditional occupations or in new areas to enable them to take up skilled and gainful occupations.

21. In addition, there is a backlog of school drop outs who have crossed the school age and are working as semi-skilled and skilled workers. The total labour force in the country in the age group of 15 to 59 consists of all these groups and is of the order of about 23.70 crores (March 1980). Of this only about 10 per cent is in the organised sector. The remaining are either employed without training, partially employed or unemployed.

22. There has not been planned educational programmes for this large population. Agencies like community polytechnics, TRYSEM, Krishi Vigyankendras, Nehru Yuvak Kendras, KVIC, Social Welfare Centres, All India Handicraft Boards, Council for Advancement of Rural Technology, etc. are not contributing to many non-formal programmes, to some extent. Concerted and well coordinated efforts are required to meet the demands of this task.

Vocational Education: Special Groups

23. The tribal and rural population do not have adequate access to school education, vocational courses in schools or vocational/technical training schools/institutions. There is also a paucity of vocational courses/institutions to cater to the

women population whose earning power could be considerably augmented through vocational training. Handicapped and disabled persons form another significant sections of the society who have at present practically no avenues to acquire suitable productive skills to make their living more meaningful and self-reliant.

Programmes

24. The policy statements concerning the system for vocationalisation have been clustered with reference to interrelated objectives, priorities and programmes into four key areas so as to ensure logical development of programmes of action, These areas include "development of the system", "vocational education programmes", "programmes for special groups" and of school population" and "targets and preparations for development".

Pre-requisites, Priorities and Guiding Principles

25. It is important to view the programme of vocationalisation at the higher secondary stage, as an important component of the overall school education both as a self-contained stage as well as feeder to the general and professional education at the tertiary stage. The management system proposed in subsequent paragraphs for the vocational effort therefore, should be seen as supportive/ complementary to the current system for the management of school education. In implementing the plan of action for vocationalisation the following guiding principles will apply:

 i) The policy clearly stipulates that a minimum of 10 per cent of students at the +2 stage should be diverted to the vocational stream by the end of the Seventh Plan. This would be achieved largely by making use of the existing set tip for administration, provision of research and development support, and certification of the vocational programmes. The existing system for this purpose will have to be suitably strengthened in order that it is functionally adequate to cope with the dimensions of the task during the Seventh Plan and could provide the nucleus for a more elaborate set-up needed for meeting greater challenges during the subsequent plans.

ii) A beginning, however, would have to be made during the Seventh Plan towards establishing the desired new structure because it will take some time for the structures to come into being and to develop professional competence and expertise for the task ahead. While the report of the National Working Group under the Chairmanship of Dr. Kulandai Swamy provides a suitable model, the principle of flexibility to suit the requirements of the respective States will be followed. It would allow the organisational structures to be modulated by the States according to the planned coverage, implementation stage of the programme, and specific local contexts. It would be desirable to involve institutions of higher education in the vicinity of the target schools in the promotion and implementation of the vocational programme.

iii) While the target in relation to the +2 stage will be fulfilled and efforts will be made to exceed the target, modest beginning will be made during this plan in the area of non-formal vocational education for drop-outs and other target groups. This will help to gain sufficient experience and expertise before undertaking expansion of the programme on larger scale in the 8th and subsequent plans. Greater accent on the +2 programme in the current plan will also create a pool of human resources needed for future expansion of vocational education both in the formal and non-formal sectors.

iv) In relation to the targets laid down in the policy for the Seventh Plan it is necessary to recognise that there is a minimum level of funding below which a meaningful programme of vocationalisation cannot be implemented. A level of funding below this critical level will not make much impact and could indeed be counter-productive by discrediting the concept of vocationalisation.

v) It is important to generate acceptability and respectability for vocationalisation of education. For this purpose: (1) Efforts will have to be made by employment sectors of the economy to create a demand for vocationally trained manpower. Agencies and sectors will be expected to identify jobs which require vocational skills and in recruitment to these jobs preference will have to be given to the graduates of the vocational programmes. It may be recognised that access to such jobs by those holding higher but vocationally irrelevant qualifications has been a strong deterrent to the vocational education effort in the past. (2) Linkages through bridge courses, modification of existing educational progra-mmes, and other measures, should create a situation for greater professional advancement of the vocat-ional graduates. Opportunities for higher education, continuing education and training will have to be created.

vi) The role of the +2 stage in schools vis-a-vis those of the polytechnics, ITIs and other certificate level institutions in providing vocational opportunities have to be outlined. While ITIs and polytechnics would cater generally to the organised industrial sector, the thrust in the school programme would be on the sectors not covered by them and on the potentially very much larger service sector. The school system would give greater attention to the areas of agriculture, agro-industries, business and commerce, home science, and health and paramedical vocations. However, this demarcation is not meant to exclude institutions from taking up vocational programmes in other areas if a need is identified and other institutional mechanisms are not available.

vii) On an average 10 additional schools will be taken up in each district by the end of Seventh plan for vocational effort at the +2 stage with a minimum intake of 40 students.

The plan of action in regard to the four areas mentioned earlier is given below.

A) Developing of the System

Developing organisational structure

26. A Joint Council for Vocational Education (JCVE) will be set up by the MHRD, to be the apex body for policy planning and coordination of vocational education at national level. In addition, a Bureau for Vocational Education will be established in the Ministry of Human Resource Development (MHRD).

27. A Central Institute of Vocational Education (CIVE) under the NCERT will be set up to perform research

and development, monitoring and evaluation functions.

28. State Government will set up appropriate bodies/ organisations like State Councils of Vocational Education (SCVE), State Institutes of Vocational Education (SIVE), Departments of vocational Education, and district-level coordination committees as per their needs and requirements.

29. Organisations like NCERT, CIVE, Regional Colleges of Education (RCE), SCERTs, SIVEs, Technical Teacher's Training Institutes (TTIs) etc., will be strengthened by providing additional infrastructure and faculty positions to perform their functions effectively for the development of vocationalisation.

30. State Councils of Vocational Education will organise district-wise needs assessment of vocational manpower, through area vocational surveys. WERT will work out a scheme for need assessment, in collaboration with organisations like SCERTs SIVEs, RCEs, TTTIs, Industry and other technical institutions.

Developing resources/facilities

31. Curriculum Development Cells/Centres will be set up in SIVEs/SCERTs and other selected professional insti-tutions in specialised fields to design vocational programmes to meet identified needs and develop curri-cula. NCERT will develop model curricula and guidelines.

32. Training of personnel for Instructional Resource Development will be organised by NCERT, SCERTs, TTTIs RCEs, CDCs, etc. the activity will be coordinated by CIVE at national level and SIVEs at state level.

33. District Vocational Training Centres will be set up by MHRD with adequate facilities to impart skill training

to vocational students in diverse vocations. Such institutions will have highly trained and skilled instructors. The facilities and faculty resources at these centres will be shared by vocational students from a number of schools in the area according to a coordinated plan.

Developing linkages

34. National Council of Educational Research and Training/ Central Institute of Vocational Education will prepare a guideline document, listing the various organisations/agencies at national/regional/ state/district levels and indicating broadly the nature of their functions and responsibilities, to develop the right kind of linkage at state and at district levels.

35. NCERT/CIVE, in collaboration with State Institutes of Vocational Education/State Councils of Educational Research and Training will evolve an information system for vocational education to ensure constant communi-cation between the central and state governments, nodal agencies, directorates, district level authorities and the institutions alongwith participating employer organisations.

36. MHRD will take steps to prepare a guideline document indicating the nature and functions of linkages between policy making bodies including Joint Council of Vocational Education, NCERT/CIVE, RCEs, TTTIs, SCERTs/SIVEs, District Coordination Committees, Research and Development Organisations in Education and Training, District Vocational Training Centres, etc., the Ministry of Human Resource Development, the Board of Apprenticeship Training, Examination and various Certification bodies including Boards of Examination.

37. State departments of vocational education will give directives and guidelines to vocational institutions to develop linkages between schools, employers and voluntary organisations in the community, to facilitate successful implementation of vocational programmes ensuring optimum resource utilisation as well as effectiveness. State departments of vocational education will prepare the scheme for the same.

B) Vocational Education Programmes

38. Vocational programmes for 8+ students will be introduced on experimental basis on a limited scale in different states, by state departments of vocational education. SCERTs/SIVEs shall develop models in the light of the guidelines laid down by JCVE and NCERT. The models already in operation shall be studied by CIVE/NCERT for deciding about the need/justification for further expansion. In engineering trade, however, the Industrial Training Institutes (ITIs) wherever considered necessary shall continue to offer vocational programmes for 8+ students.

39. Programmes at 10+ level will be formulated by SCERTs/ SIVEs in the light of guidelines laid down by NCERT. The SCVEs shall facilitate the introduction of these programmes on the basis of result of area vocational surveys in selected schools in a phased manner keeping in view the national targets.

40. To provide more opportunities to students for 10+ vocational courses in engineering and technology, 100 more vocational institutions shall be established.

41. JCVE will provide in a phased manner 70 per cent of the higher secondary vocational stream graduates stipend to undergo paid apprenticeship in appropriate industries. The implementation will be

carried out by Regional Boards of Apprenticeship Training in collaboration with state departments of vocational education, and other concerned agencies.

42. Tertiary level programme like Diploma in Vocational subjects, Advanced Diploma Programmes, and Degree Programmes will be introduced in selected polytechnics, affiliated colleges and universities, as well as in special Institutes set up for this purpose. JCVE and SCVEs shall develop schemes for creating such tertiary level vocational education facilities at non-university institutions. For the university level courses, the universities will develop model curricula in collaboration with NCERT/CIVE for starting programmes in vocational education at university departments and affiliated colleges.

43. Entrepreneurial/self-employment skills will be developed in vocational stream students, through curriculum, special training programmes as well as paid apprenticeship facilities.

44. State departments of vocational education and SCVEs will formulate necessary schemes for the purpose.

45. State directorates of vocational education will set tip career guidance cells at district level. NCERT/CIVE shall formulate suitable norms for the purpose.

46. NCERT/CIVE, SCERTs/SIVEs, RCEs, CDC, TTTIs and other institutes will develop bridge/transfer courses in accordance with the guidelines laid down by JCVE. Suitable schemes for course offering shall be developed by SCVEs.

C) Programmes for Special Groups and out of School

Population: involving industry/community

47. JCVE will evolve schemes to involve the public/

private sector industry in vocational education through appropriate incentives/rewards. Also, JCVE would arrange to bring about appropriate legislation to ensure their contribution.

48. JCVE/SCVEs/State departments of vocational education will identify and support voluntary organisations engaged in the vocational education of special groups like women, tribals, handicapped and disabled, etc. Suitable scheme for this will be formulated by JCVE.

Non-formal Programmes

49. All polytechnic institutions, ITIs, other vocational and technical training institutions, selected higher secondary schools, colleges and special institutes will engage themselves in imparting vocational education through non-formal programmes, to the rural and unorganised sector in a phased manner. Suitable schemes for the purpose, like the Community Polytechnic Scheme, will be formulated by JCVE for respective categories of institutions.

50. Selected engineering colleges, polytechnics, Industrial Training Institutes and other Vocational and Technical Training Schools/Institutes will engage themselves in conducting part time vocational course for the benefit of special groups and those already employed. State departments of vocational education will formulate necessary schemes for the purpose and promote their implementation. A suitable scheme for undertaking such activities in selected institutions will also be formulated by JCVE.

Setting-up special institutes

51. Special vocational training institutes for women,

tribals and other weaker sections of the society to meet identified needs, will be established by the State departments of vocational education.

52. Centres for vocational training of the handicapped will be set up in institutions like special institutes of relevant/useful technology, District Vocational Training Centres, ITIs and Polytechnics to equip this section of the society with appropriate employable skills. State Departments of Vocational Education will formulate necessary schemes for the purpose and promote their impleme-ntation through them and/or other concerned depart-ments. JCVE will formulate a central scheme for establishing such units.

D) Targets and Preparation for Development Targets

53. For 10 per cent diversion by 1990, provision will have to be made for 2.5 lakhs. In view of the action already taken, additional requirements for 2.5 lakh students can be met by marginal expansion of the infrastructure and resources but for 25 per cent diversion by 1995 advance action will to be taken by the States and Central Governments in terms of building a requisite level of infrastructure and facilities.

Teacher Training

54. A phased and coordinated programme or the training of teachers, principals and key officials in the vocational education system using the available infrastructures in organisations like NCERT, RCE, SIVEs, TTTIs, CDCs, State Institutes of Education, will be undertaken. Scheme will be drawn up by concerned institutions in accordance with guidelines given by JCVE. Crash programmes will also be organised by concerned institutions to meet the immediate

requirements for which a scheme shall be formulated by JCVE.

55. NCERT/CIVE and SCERT/SIVEs will evolve and implement phased programme for the development of textbooks and other instructional materials on a large scale to meet the diverse needs of a variety of vocational programmes and to avoid duplication of efforts to the extent possible. JCVE/SCVE will formulate suitable guidelines for the same.

56. State department of vocational education will evolve schemes to utilise community resources, both in terms of part-time teachers and by way of training facilities in industries, KVIC, KRKs, farms, etc., to enhance the quality of instruction.

Facilitating Employment

57. Steps will be taken to change recruitment rules for selection to Government departments at Central and State levels and Public Sector in order to give due weightage to vocational stream graduates ill posts appropriate to their vocations.

58. A Monitoring and Evaluation Cell in the Bureau of Vocational Education will be set up with appropriate linkages to CIVE/NCERT, SIVE/SCERT and other agencies involved to facilitate implementation.

59. NCERT/CIVE and SCERT/SIVE will formulate schemes for periodic review of vocational programmes in accordance with the general guidelines laid down by JCVE.

3

Planning of Elementary Education

In its endeavour to build a just and humane society, the Indian government has resolved to make the right to elementary education a fundamental right and to enforce it through suitable statutory measures.

The resolve is expected to help remove obstacles in achieving UEE. It has several positive aspects:

— The Constitutional enactment for the right to education would demonstrate the necessary political will and administrative resolve of the country to achieve UEE and eradication of illiteracy.

— The legislation would spur the governmental and non- governmental sectors to take necessary measures to provide universal access to elementary education and to ensure universal retention and achievement.

— The provision for making elementary education a fundamental right would create the required pressure on the central and state governments to focus on the special needs of the undeserved and unserved population and regions.

— The government's commitment to provide 6 % of GDP for education and to earmark 50 % for primary education should provide the requisite financial back up and support to the constitutional enactment.

— Revitalisation of Panchayati Raj Institutions (PRIs), in the wake of the 73rd constitutional amendment, provides an opportunity to bring about effective devolution and decentralisation of authority for planning and management of elementary education to give effect to the constitutional enactment.

— The proposal is expected to have a positive impact on eradication of child labour.

— The spread of elementary education would have a good impact on other social indicators like population growth, health and women's development, as well as enhancement of productivity of the economy and reduction in unemployment.

The extent to which the proposed right will bear fruit will depend on the ability of the state governments to finance education, and the resources raised through the Finance and Planning Commissions; the priority accorded to competing demands in the social sector; as well as expenditure of the household sector on education. On the other hand, it is realised that legislation in relation to compulsory education should ensure that penalties against parents ought only to serve as a deterrent and should be enforced as a last resort and that too in a compassionate and humane manner.

State governments have abolished tuition fees in government schools till the upper primary level. Education in schools run by local bodies and private aided institutions.

Article 45 of the Constitution of India directs that the Sate shall endeavour to provide within a period of 10 years from the commencement of the Constitution, free and compulsory education for all children until they complete the age of 14 years.

The government has now resolved to translate this directive into a fundamental right of every child between

6 to 14 years of age. This would give a further fillip to the nation's efforts to achieve UEE.

are also mostly free. However, unaided institutions of elementary education do charge tuition and other fees. Other costs of education such as textbooks, stationery, uniforms, school bags and transportation are generally met by parents. State governments provide text books and uniforms, as incentives for children from Scheduled Castes/ Scheduled Tribes (SC/ST) and girls at the primary level.

The Compulsory Education legislation have been enacted in 14 states and 4 union territories. These have remained unenforced due to various socioeconomic and cultural factors as well as administrative and financial constraints.

The Government of India has not enacted any legislation in this regard so far, as it holds the opinion that the compulsion contemplated in Article 45 of the Constitution is on the state rather than on the parents and children. It has, therefore, been advocating a consensual approach to motivate parents and children. The key elements of this approach have been:

— Community involvement.
— Decentralisation of planning and management of school education to PRIs.
— Motivation of children to attend schools regularly.
— Improvement -of infrastructure and facilities in. schools.
— Development of locally relevant curricula.
— Improvement in quality of textbooks.
— Teacher training.
— Child centred learning.
— Adoption of minimum levels of learning.

The government would continue to strengthen the consensual approach and social mobilisation for UEE. The constitutional enactment is expected to provide further momentum to the nation's efforts to achieve UEE at a faster pace.

STATUS OF ELEMENTARY EDUCATION THE ROAD TRAVERSED

UEE has been accepted as a national goal since 1950. It implies universal access, retention and achievement of children in classes I to VIII. Concretely this means:

Universal Access: Universal enrolment of all children, including disadvantaged children; provision of a primary school within 1 km. walking distance and facilities for nonformal education for school dropouts, working children and girls who cannot attend formal schools; and improvement in the ratio of upper primary schools to primary schools from the existing level of 1:4 to 1:2.

Universal Retention: Reduction of dropout rates in classes I-V and class VI-VIII from the current levels of 46 % and 60 % respectively to 20 % and 40 % respectively.

Universal Achievement: Achievement of MLLs by almost all children at the primary level and introduction of this concept at the upper primary stage.

Within these parameters, the government is making all out efforts to honour the declarations made for achieving the goal of EFA in the Jomtien Global Conference on Basic Education in 1990, and the resolutions adopted in the Conference of the nine most populous countries (EFA-9) in 1993 at New Delhi. The national commitment to provide 6 % of GDP for education and to earmark 50 % of budgetary allocations for primary education should provide the requisite fillip to India's efforts to achieve UEE.

The rejuvenation of local bodies in most parts of the country in the wake of the 73rd and 74th constitutional amendments as well as the infusion of a large number of women members and representatives of other disadvantaged sections into these bodies have provided a great opportunity to bring about effective devolution of powers and decentralisation of authority for better planning and management of elementary education at the grassroots.

Achievements

Expanding Access: Concerted efforts towards UEE have resulted in manyfold increase in institutions, teachers and students. Between 1990-91 and 1995-96, the number of primary schools increased by 5 %. The number of upper primary schools increased by 13 %. Growth in enrolments have also been significant. It was 12 % in primary classes (I-V) and 20 % in upper primary classes (VI-VIII). Recent levels indicate that gender and sectional gaps in enrolments at the primary level are narrowing down, albeit gradually.

Retention: The dropout rates have shown a declining trend during the past four years, 1992-96. They declined from 42% in 1991-92 to 34.5% in 1995-96 in case of primary classes, showing an overall decrease of 7.5 %. In case of upper primary classes, the dropout rates declined by 7.1% from 58.7% in 1991-92 to 51.6% in 1995-96.

Learner's Achievement: One of the thrust areas of UEE has been the effort to improve learning achievement of children both in primary and upper primary classes, mainly through the programme of Minimum Levels of Learning (MLLs). Several states have successfully used the idea of MLL to launch a number of activities including revision of text books, changes in curricula and teaching Methodologies, as well as the content of teacher training.

Despite significant achievements in UEE, there are severe gender, regional, sectional and caste disparities in UEE. A significant proportion of students-dropout due to socioeconomic and cultural factors as also due to lack of adequate infrastructure, shortage of teachers and other reasons. A large proportion of children in the 6- 14 age group are out of school.

Ensuring access to good quality learning environment for all children in the age group of 6-14 is still a daunting task. The nation has taken up this challenge. As India enters the next 5 years of planned development, straddling across to the next century midway, it stands committed to achieve UEE.

Elementary Education Initiatives

Since independence, the central and state governments have been expanding the provision of primary formal and non-formal education to realise the goal of UEE. The challenge now is to sustain and deepen current reforms in education and encourage local planning and management of strategies for expanding and improving primary education.

With a view to cushioning the impact of rising costs of text books and exercise books, the government has exempted writing and printing paper supplied to all State Text Book Corporations from excise duty. It is expected that this would make school text books more affordable for students from weaker sections of society.

Removal of systemic deficiencies in the implementation of UEE and forging ahead necessitates the creation of informed public opinion and a facilitative environment akin to that of the Total Literacy Campaign. This has to be achieved through effective and sustained advocacy, massive community mobilisation and consciousness building. With this perspective, a national programme of media publicity and advocacy has been planned. The programme will target: i) teachers and all those involved in education of children; ii) students and parents of students, particularly non-literate parents; and iii) community opinion leaders.

The Kasturba Gandhi Shiksha Yojana, a programme to establish residential schools for girls in all the districts which have a particularly low female literacy rate has been announced. A sum of Rs. 2500 million has been provided in this year's budget. The central government has also decided to grant financial incentives and scholarships for the girl child born in families living below the poverty line.

Several central and state level initiatives have been in operation from the early 1980s. While the design of these projects vary substantially, all of them address the objectives and strategies of the National Policy on Education 1986. They pay special attention to increasing girls' enrolment, improving educational outcomes, strengthening community involvement, improving teaching and learning materials and providing in-service teacher training. The status of some of these initiatives are discussed below.

Operation Blackboard

This scheme launched in 1987, is aimed at improving the school environment and enhancing retention and learning achievement of children by providing minimum essential facilities in all primary schools. The scheme has brought about a remarkable quantitative and qualitative improvement in primary education. In all, 523,000 primary schools have been covered as originally envisaged. These schools have been provided with central assistance.

Decentralisation

Decentralised planning and management of elementary education is a goal set by the National Policy on Education, 1986. The Policy visualises direct community involvement in the form of Village Education Committees (VECs) for management of elementary education. The POA, 1992, emphasised microplanning as a process of designing a family-wise and child-wise plan of action by which every child regularly attends school or NFE centre, continues his or her education at the place suitable to him/her and completes at least eight years of schooling or its equivalent at the NFE centre.

The 73rd and 74th constitutional amendments provide for decentralisation of the activities and facilitate transfer of power and participation of the local self-government institutions or the Panchayati Raj Institutions. It has created a congenial ambience for the PRIs to play a more dynamic and proactive role. States are expected to evolve institutional arrangements both in rural and urban areas for undertaking these activities. These structures have been providing voice to women, Scheduled Castes and Tribes, minorities, parents and educational functionaries. They have also, been delegated with responsibilities with regard to location and relocation of existing primary and upper schools on the basis of microplanning and school mapping. In this regard, decentralisation of school management to grassroots level bodies is an important policy initiative.

During the 8th plan period several innovative efforts hove been made under the ongoing projects to establish decentralisation. For instance, the District Primary Education Programme has shifted the planning mechanism from the state to the district level, and Lok Jumbish has gone one step further by assigning decision making processes to a block level committee. At the village level, a VEC has the main responsibility for community mobilisation, school mapping, microplanning, renovation and construction of school buildings and improvement of pedagogical curriculum. In fact, the VECs of Shiksha Karmi schools have been activated as a result of the Lok Jumbish programme of Rs. 10,000 each for teaching learning equipment. Near about 147,000 single teacher schools have been upgraded to dual teacher schools. Construction of 174,000 classrooms has been undertaken with central assistance and contributions from the concerned states.

Since 1993-94, the scheme has been expanded to cover upper primary schools. More then 47,000 upper primary schools have been granted central assistance of Rs. 40,000 each for purchase of teaching- learning materials. Also, primary schools with enrolment exceeding 100 have been augmented with a third teacher. A Special Orientation Programme for Primary Teachers (SOPT) to facilitate optimum utilisation of materials supplied has also been launched to cover all primary school teachers in the country.

The total expenditure under the scheme from 1992-93 to 1995-96 has been Rs. 8,163 million. The outlay for 1996-97 is Rs. 2,910 million.

National Programme of Nutritional Support to Primary Education (School Meal Programme)

This scheme was launched on 15 August, 1995 to give a boost to UEE in terms of increasing enrolment, retention and attendance in primary classes by supplementing nutritional requirements of children attending primary schools. It is an ambitious scheme that has been operationalised throughout the country in a very short period. The programme envisages provision of nutritious and wholesome cooked meal of 100 gms of foodgrains per school day, free of cost, to all children in classes I-V by 1997-98.

During 1995-96, 378 districts, 225,000 schools and 33.5 million children have been covered with an expenditure of Rs. 4,412 million. In 1996-97, the scheme was extended to cover 55.4 million children with an expenditure of Rs. 8,110 million. The scheme has become fully operational in 1997-98 covering nearly 110 million children in primary classes. A positive impact on school enrolment and retention has been reported.

District Primary Education Programme

The DPEP launched in November, 1994 is conceived as a beachhead for overhauling the primary education system in India. The programme aims at operationalising the strategies for achieving UEE through district specific planning and disaggregated target setting. It draws upon the accumulated national experience of several state level initiatives that were started earlier. It moves away from the schematic piecemeal approach of the earlier programmes and takes a holistic view of primary education with emphasis on decentralised management, community mobilisation and district specific planning based on contextuality and research based inputs.

Objectivcs of DPEP

The basic objectives of DPEP are:

— To provide all children with access to primary education either in the formal system or through the non-formal education (NFE) programme.

— To reduce differences in enrolment, dropout rates and learning achievement among gender and social groups to less than 5%.

— To reduce overall primary dropout rates for all students to less than 10%.

— To raise average achievement levels by at least 25% over measured base line levels and ensuring achievements of basic literacy and numeracy competencies and a minimum of 40% achievement levels in other competencies by all primary school children.

The Government of India finances 85 % of the project cost as a grant to the DPEP State Implementation Societies and the concerned state government provides the rest. The central government's share is resourced by external funding. As of now, IDA has approved credit amounting to $260 million and $425 million under Phase-I and Phase-II respectively. The European Union (EU) is providing a grant of 150 million ECU. The ODA (UK) is extending a grant of $80.21 million. The grant from the Netherlands amounts to $25.8 million.

The first phase of the programme was launched in 42 districts in the states of Assam, Haryana, Karnataka, Kerala, Maharashtra, Tamilnadu and Madhya Pradesh. In the second phase, the programme has been launched in 80 districts of Orissa, Himachal Pradesh, Andhra Pradesh, West Bengal, Uttar Pradesh and Gujarat and in Phase I States.

During the last three years, DPEP has been able to set up project management structures at district, state and national levels, create the environment and capacity for microplanning, take up the challenge of pedagogical innovation, create a responsive institutional base which includes both government and non-government institutions, enhance community participation and strengthen the process of catering to special focus groups such as tribals, scheduled castes, women and other marginalised sections.

The first phase of the programme is under evaluation. The initial trends of impact studies are very positive. DPEP has made a decisive impact on increasing enrolment, reducing repetition rates and improving class room processes.

While the DPEP has been targeting backward districts with female literacy below the national average and where TLCs have stirred up a demand for elementary education, several state level initiatives have shown tremendous potential. These are directed at improving literacy levels in the five low literacy states of Andhra Pradesh, Bihar, Uttar Pradesh, Madhya Pradesh and Rajasthan.

Bihar Education Project

Bihar Education Project (BEP) was launched in 1991 with the express purpose of bringing about quantitative and qualitative improvement in the elementary system in Bihar.

The project lays emphasis on the education of deprived sections of society, such as SCs, STs and women. Participatory planning and implementation are crucial ingredients of the project.

A midterm review highlighted certain major achievements such as: a) a strong Mahila Samakhya component; b) organisation of VECs and community involvement in programme implementation at grassroot level; and c) non-formal education through NGOs. The review suggested:

— consolidation of the programme in the existing seven districts,

— establishing strong linkages between BEP and the education system in Bihar,

— giving greater focus to the primary stage of classes I-V,
— building better linkages with the activities in other states under DPEP and other programmes,
— providing more emphasis to MLLs and teacher training, and conducting periodic base line studies.

It has now been decided to extend the project to the second phase of two years duration. The total outlay for the second phase is estimated to be Rs. 613 million to be shared between UNICEF, Government of India and Government of Bihar as per the existing funding formula of 3:2:1. The total project outlay for BEP is Rs. 3600 million. It is proposed to merge the project with DPEP during the next five years.

Uttar Pradesh Basic Education Programme

A project "Education for All" prepared by the Government of Uttar Pradesh was approved by The World Bank in June, 1993. The project is currently in operation in 12 districts. It is planned to expand the coverage to 15 districts under DPEP-II. It has an outlay of Rs. 7,288 million spread over seven years. International Development Agency (IDA), the soft loan window of The World Bank, would provide a credit of US$163.1 million and the state government's share would be approximately 13 per cent of the total project cost.

The progress of implementation of the project so far has been satisfactory. The construction work of schools and Block Resource Centres is being completed as per schedule. Training materials for teacher trainers on DIETs have been prepared. The first cycle of in- service teacher training was completed in October, 1995. About 40,000 teachers have been trained.

Community Mobilisation and Participation

Many educational innovations of recent years are based on the strong foundation of community support and participation. When progress is discussed and analysed of different levels within the project, "people's acceptance and participation" is used as an indicator.

Mobilising the village community to take responsibility to ensure quality education for every child, is the core strategy of both Lok Jumbish (LJ) and Shikhsa Karmi Project (SKP) in their efforts to universalise primary education and deliver quality education. It would not be far removed from truth if we say that community involvement has been the key factor for the success of the two projects.

LJ has had a positive effect on the empowerment of locally elected people, especially on female representatives at village level, who are often active members of the LJ core teams or women's groups. The Village Education Committees(VECs), carefully formed and trained though environmental building activities in the LJ programme, are actively involved in school matters.

SKP has constituted VECs in 2000 villages to promote community involvement in primary education and encourage village level planning. The role of the VEC is to mobilise resources for maintenance, repair and construction of school infrastructure. The VEC also helps in determining the school calendar and school timings in consultation with the local community and Shiksha Karmis (educational workers).

The positive impact of the LJ and SKP, focusing on supporting the teachers and the students by involving, the village community in taking responsibility for all educational activities of the village school, is serving as a demonstration of how deeply rooted problems of education in India can be addressed. Wide dissemination of these innovative approaches could inspire other educational programmes all over India and the world.

Andhra Pradesh Primary Education Project

The Andhra Pradesh Primary Education Project (APPEP), practised in the south central state of Andhra Pradesh, with a female literacy of just 34 %, adopts a two-pronged strategy of improving classroom transaction by training teachers and giving a fillip to school construction activities. The project has trained an estimated 80,000 teachers in 23 districts and more than 3,000 teaching centres have become operational. The project is assisted by the ODA with an estimated outlay of Rs. 1,000 million in the 8th Plan.

Shiksha Karmi Project

The Shiksha Karmi Project (SKP) is being implemented since 1987, with assistance from the Swedish International Development Cooperation Agency (SIDA). The project aims at universalisation and qualitative improvement of primary education in the remote and socioeconomically backward villages of Rajasthan, with primary focus on girls. Since teacher absenteeism has been found to be a major obstacle in achieving the objective of UEE, the project uses the novel approach of substituting teachers in dysfunctional schools with local youth known as Shiksha Karmis who are provided with rigorous training and supervisory support. An important feature of this innovative project is the mobilisation and participation of the community in improving the functioning of primary schools.

The project is being implemented as an externally aided scheme with reimbursement of 90 % in Phase I and 50 % in Phase II, from SIDA. The project, with an outlay of around Rs.212 million in Phase I and Rs.490 million in Phase II, places strong emphasis on vigorous and continuous in-service training.

The SKP also runs non-formal classes called Prehar Pathshalas-schools of convenient timings. For girls' education, Angan Pathshalas are being run in three blocks. The programme at present covers over 150,000 students in 1,785 schools and 3,520 Prehar Pathshalas, involving over 4,271 Shiksha Karmis.

The project is known for its open participative style and continuous experimentation to achieve its objectives. The approach, strategies and achievements of the SKP have attracted national and international recognition. The project is slated for a major expansion with SIDA assistance in the 9th Plan. The total projections for the 9th Plan are estimated to be Rs. 4260 million.

Lok Jumbish Project

Barely five years old, Lok Jumbish (LJ) has made an indelible impression in the primary education landscape of Rajasthan. The coverage of the project has extended to 75 blocks, covering a population of approximately 12 million. Significantly, it has also achieved a major breakthrough in welding together government agencies, teachers, NGOs, elected representatives and the people into an interactive group effort to promote universalisation of primary education. The seven guiding principles of Lok Jumbish are:

— a process rather than a product approach;

— partnerships;

— decentralised functioning;

— participatory learning;

— integration with the mainstream education system;

— flexibility of management; and
— creating multiple levels of leadership committed to quality and mission mode.

Special focus has been given to environment building in all training programmes under LJ. This helps in the development of an understanding about issues involved in people's mobilisation, use of different media forms and clarity about the messages to be given to the people.

The first phase of the project was for a period of two years from 1992-94, with the expenditure shared between SIDA, Government of India and Government of Rajasthan in the ratio 3:2:1. The second phase stretches up to 1998, with the sharing modality remaining the same. The allocation for LJP is Rs.1100 million for Phases I and II and Rs.4000 million for Phase III. A Norwegian grant of Rs. 200 million is also available.

Sahaj Shiksha Programme (SSP) was started in LJ (as NFE) in June 1993. A programme evaluation conducted after two years has observed that 96% of the NFE centres were functioning efficiently, the level of motivation among instructors and learners was high, there was a high degree of community involvement in the programmes and that the level of achievement of the learners were comparable with the formal school system.

A significant area which reflects LJ's concern for gender equity is the content and process of education. Steps have been initiated to incorporate gender equity in curriculum and textbooks. The faculty of Lok Jumbish is working in close cooperation with Sandhan, an NGO, in this area.

The buildings development programme of LJ is beginning to have an impact on the Government of Rajasthan with respect to its school buildings programme. LJ designs have been accepted and widely disseminated.

LJ has some remarkable achievements to its credit. The style of partnership between LJ and NGOs has been emulated by other programmes and their stress on gender equity and women's development is a harbinger of similar efforts elsewhere. LJ's achievement in enhancing enrolment and retention have been widely acclaimed, as also the impact on achievement levels.

Joyful Learning and Teaching

Shikshak Samakhya, or Teacher Empowerment Strategy, now being implemented in modified forms as Joyful Learning/Teaching in several Indian states as an in-service teacher training strategy for mobilising teachers on a mass scale, is an unprecedented story of success and innovation within the Indian subcontinent. This programme, underway in 11 states of India, has created a revolution in the nature of teacher training and has stressed on the importance of participatory approaches and mobilisation techniques in teacher training programmes.

Pivotal to the success of the teacher empowerment programme in India is its use of the participatory approach for training, design and implementation. It essentially draws on teacher resources from the district, block and cluster levels, aimed at empowering the teacher to make their own decisions. Teachers are involved in highly participatory sessions from the initial stages of designing the content of the training package, to the actual training sessions delivered by core trainers selected mainly from the teachers themselves.

The most powerful aspect of joyful learning programmes are that they provide an extremely effective teacher mobilisation strategy which leads to highly motivated and transformed teachers in a very short time. Teachers take a pledge to change their role and to make the classroom a joyful and stimulating learning environment and to do so together with leaders from the community as well as educational functionaries. A further incentive for change has been the participation of teachers in making their own teaching aids, their involvement in the writing of handbooks and worksheets, their involvement in the organisation of the training programme in the various blocks and its extension to the cluster level training, and their active cooperation in using their own creative talents in the design of activities, songs, drama and dances to accompany the various MLL competencies.

The teacher empowerment programme represents a macro-approach towards mobilising teachers on a large scale and has expanded rapidly into new districts. Attempts are now directed towards analysing teacher competencies and training needs to arrive at a comprehensive, recurrent and sustainable in-service training programme.

One of the specific joyful Learning initiative is the Guru Mitra, which was launched by the Government of Rajasthan in collaboration with UNICEF in 1994. By the beginning of 1997, 38 blocks in 10 districts have been covered under this initiative. Guru, the teacher is the pivot of this initiative. The project is a joint endeavour of teachers, parents, community, PRIs and administrators to strengthen UPE. Guru Mitra offers conditions for a teacher to learn from fellow teachers in MLL-based joyful learning during the foundation training course followed by. monthly cluster level enrichment sessions.

National Elementary Education Mission

In view of the rapid expansion of the elementary education system and the emerging challenges, the government is contemplating several structural changes of national and state levels for achieving the good of UEE. Within this background, the commitment made in the revised NPE, 1992, for launching a National Elementary Education Mission (NEEM) is being given final shape. A major task before such a Mission would be to evolve strategies for reaching the unreached and achieving the goals of UEE within a given time frame in a systematic, sustained and integrated manner by involving all segments of civil society in this national endeavour. The objectives of the Mission will be:

— Universal access and enrolment;

— Universal retention of children up to 14 years of age; and

— a substantial improvement in the quality of education to enable all children to achieve essential levels of learning.

The approach and strategy of the Mission would incorporate the following rents:

— genuine and effective involvement and participation of all people- Political parties, mass organisations, trade unions, peasants, youth groups, women's collectives, individuals, and social activists so as to make UEE a mass movement.

— national arousal and social mobilisation through media- print,theatre, fold culture and kala jathas.

— a time bound and decentralised perspective with rigorous planning at district, block and cluster levels for achieving the goal of UEE;

— accountability and transparency at all levels of the elementary education system.

The political resolve to make the right to elementary education a fundamental right has cast a greater responsibility on the Government to achieve UEE. The national Elementary Education Mission is expected to play the role of an overarching body to meet this challenge.

Community Based Primary Education:

To provide programme support in a coordinated manner to the ongoing efforts of the Government of India (GOI) towards the goal of Universalisation of Elementary Education, the joint GOI-UN System for Support for Community Based Primary Education has been slated for a major takeoff. It is a collaborative effort of the GOI and five UN agencies namely, UNICEF, UNDP, ILO, UNESCO and UNFPA. The programme aims at enhancing the capacity for community participation in effective school management, improving the performance of primary school teachers for the use of interactive, childcentred and gender- sensitive methods of teaching in multigrade classrooms and addressing social factors which affect the attendance and performance of school-age children adversely.

The programme is likely to become operational in eight states, namely, Andhra Pradesh, Bihar, Karnataka, Madhya Pradesh, Maharashtra, Orissa, Rajasthan and Uttar Pradesh from the year 1998.

Early Childhood Care

While the process of human development is essentially cumulative in nature, the first six years of a child's life are the most critical for his/her development. Thus, investment in programmes for the youngest children in the range of 0-6 years becomes a major priority as the very foundation for basic education and lifelong learning and development.

The all important significance of Early Childhood Care and Education (ECCE) is compensation for early childhood deprivations at the home front by providing an appropriately stimulating environment to the children in the areas of health and education. Quality ECE (Early Childhood Education) programmes, a major component of ECCE, have demonstrated a positive impact on retention rates and achievement levels in primary grades.

While most of the coverage under ECCE in India is carried out through the ICDS scheme, other pre-primary and day-care centres are also involved.

Integrated Child Development Services

ICDS is the largest ECCE programme, at present, in the country. It is an intersectoral programme, which reaches out to children from vulnerable and remote areas. The scheme's package of services includes:

— supplementary nutrition

— immunisation

— health checkups referral services

— non-formal preschool education nutrition and health education; for children below six years, and pregnant and nursing mothers.

The 8th Plan period saw the accelerated expansion of ICDS, with the total number of blocks under coverage being 3,072 in the first three years. The ICDS scheme was universalised in 1995-96, through the sanction of projects for all the 5,320 community development blocks and 310 major urban slums. This led to an increase in the total number of anganwadi centres to 0.4 million.

Presently, ICDS reaches 10.63 million children (in the age-group of 3- 6) with its preschool facility. Although the scheme has now expanded and been made more accessible, it is felt that the preschool component needs further strengthening. Towards this end, a monitoring system has been devised to focus on this area; the training curriculum of the different levels of ICDS functionaries has been revised; and the process of the selection of core material for anganwadi centres and supervisory personnel is on, to further strengthen their capabilities. Instructions to the states have also been issued for teachers of primary schools to visit the anganwadi centres for better coordination. This would relieve the girl child from the burden of taking care of younger siblings.

Creches and Day Care Centres Scheme

Custodial in nature, the scheme provides day care services for children (below 5 years) of casual, migrant, agricultural, and construction labourers. 12,470 creches under the scheme cater to 300,000 children. In addition to this, under the National Creche Fund, 642 creches and 150 anganwadi-cum-creches, covering about 20,000 children have been set up.

Early Childhood Education Scheme

The scheme, introduced to reduce the dropout rate in primary schools, provides central assistance to voluntary organisations for running preschool centres. With the universalisation of ICDS, ECE and also Balwadi Nutrition Programme were expected to be phased out, by the end of the 8th Plan, with their centres being merged with ICDS.

Future Strategies

While the previous plan period witnessed a quantum leap in ECCE services, primarily through ICDS, the component of ECE has only received divided attention. However, the significance of ECCE for Universalisation of Education (UEE) makes it imperative for ECE to be regarded as the first indispensable step in the educational continuum. Future efforts to achieve the same are underlined below:

— *Priority to ECE in the education sector:* This priority would be translated into action aimed at building resource capacity in ECE at all levels of the existing institutional structures in the education sector which can facilitate qualitative improvement of the ECE programmes at the field level.

— *Provision of Basic Minimum Resources:* Budgetary allocations for ECE programmes would be in conformity with Minimum Specifications for Preschools produced by NCERT, which delineates the minimum resources required for a quality programme.

— *Advocacy:* To ensure developmentally appropriate play- based programmes in ECCE, for all children, an appropriate climate and a strong parent lobby would be developed.

— *Regulation and Monitoring of Quality:* The quality of working practices propagated by the private ECE centres would be regulated by legal and persuasive measures.

— *Training:* All levels of functionaries would be provided with resource capacity building for planning, implementation and monitoring the standard ECE curriculum.

— *Strengthening of ECCE-Primary Linkage:* In the context of ECCE's crucial significance for UEE, linkages between ECE and primary education initiated in the previous plan will be strengthened in both operational and programmatic terms.

— *Micro and Need-Specific Planning:* The ECE programme would ensure flexible response to local patterns of women's work, child-care needs and local culture-specific practices.

— *Partnership with NGOs:* The participation of NGOs provides resource support for qualitative strengthening of the programmes and would be encouraged for the further development of ECCE.

— *Research:* Action research in the area of ECCE would be promoted to assess the relative long-term impact of ECE on the subsequent development and achievements of children vis-a-vis the goals of UEE.

Equal Educational Opportunities

It is very imperative that education, if it is to fulfill its potential as a decisive intervention towards social equity, must move beyond the domain of literacy to create an environment where girls, women, working children, disabled persons and persons belonging to scheduled castes, scheduled tribes and minorities are enabled to come together to explore their situations, recognise and affirm their own strengths and capacities, and act to bring about change. towards this end, all aspects of planning and implementation of educational programmes have been incorporated with a perspective that envisages enhanced participation of these groups.

Girls' and Women's Education

Women and young girls, all over the world, carry a historic burden of inequality which is visible in every aspect of their lives-in their share in the population, in the economy, in social and political life, in their access to health, information and all other aspects of development. Their educational status holds a mirror to the larger realities of their lives. There has been an increasing recognition of the fact that while UEE is the ultimate goal, no strategy can succeed without addressing its gender and class dimensions specifically.

States have exempted girls from payment of tuition fees up to graduate level. Other measures for promotion of girls' education include provision of scholarships, free text books, uniforms, attendance incentives, separate girls' schools, construction of toilets for girls and increasing proportion of women teachers in primary schools.

Participation of girls in primary education has improved significantly. Girls enrolment ratio at the primary level has increased from 5.4 in 1950-51 to 47.4 in 1995-96.

Though girls' enrolment has been outpacing that of the boys, there still exists a big gap in gender achievements. The sixth All India Educational Survey supports the contention that girls, particularly in rural areas, are the single most important group required focused attention for achievement of UEE. Recognising this, most programmes have specific components for ameliorating the conditions of the girls children and women. Some gender specific interventions are:

— Mahila Samakhya, one of the most successful efforts to link women's empowerment with education, has expanded its coverage to 35 districts.

— The TLC has been successful in raising the demand for educations, especially among women. In most of the 417 districts, women make up over 60% of adults enrolled in the programme.

— Under the scheme of Operation Blackboard, of the 147,000 teachers appointed, 47% were women.

Mahila Samakhya Project

Mahila Samakhya (MS), which means women's equality

through education, is a women's equality through education, is a women's empowerment project which aims not only at service delivery but seeks to bring about a change in women's perception about themselves and that of society in regard to their 'traditional roles'. It endeavours to create an environment for women to seek knowledge and information in order to made informed choices and create circumstances in which they can learn at their own pace and rhythm. The centrality of education in the struggle to achieve equality is an important focus of Mahila Samakhya.

The process of mobilising and organising women is facilitated by a "sahayogini" (a cluster coordinator in 10 villages). She is a crucial link between the village sangha and the district implementation unit of the programme. The latter provides resource support and inputs to meet the needs of the women. The district units are supported by a state office. At the state level, an autonomous registered society, as an empowered body, has been set up to oversee the programme. At the national level, the programme is coordinated by a Project Director. A National Resource Group-an advisory body of eminent women activists, academics, development workers and bureaucrats-supports the programme, providing it with new concepts, ideas and experiences.

The programme is operational in 5000 villages spread over 35 districts in seven states. The Mahila Samakhya was launched in March 1989 as a pilot project through Dutch assistance in 10 districts of Uttar Pradesh, Gujarat and Karnataka. In 1992, the programme was extended to Andhra Pradesh. The Mahila Samakhya approach and strategy has been further extended through other basic education programme in three districts each of Madhya Pradesh and Assam. The UP Basic Education Project is also assisting MS expansion in Uttar Pradesh.

— Non-formal Education centres run exclusively for girls get 90% assistance from the central government. number of such centres has been increased from to 40% during the 8th Plan.

— In Navodaya Vidyalayas-pace setting schools for talented rural children-at least one third of the students are girls.

— The DPEP has been targeting educationally backward districts which have a female literacy rate below the national average.

— Internationally assisted projects-SKP, LJP-have made gender issues a focus of their attention.

The programmes of elementary education though acknowledging girls as the single most important group requiring greater attention, have to be further strengthened to adequately address the many needs, risks and fears of girls and their families. The 9th Plan is expected to give greater attention and direct more funds to meet the special needs of girls. In addition to existing schemes, states will be encouraged to:

— promote formation of village level women's collectives and train local women activists to catalyse collective actions around educational issues;

— empower local bodies such as VECs, Mother-Teacher Associations and women's groups;

— build capacity of existing women's organisations/ institutions in rural areas;

— encourage women representatives in PRIs to take up school mapping and microplanning activities; and

— mobilise informed and active women's participation to build and sustain an environment supportive of girls' education.

Gender Perspective in other Programme

In line with the broad objectives of the NPE, 1986, the various educational schemes have specific gender components for the promotion of girls' and women's education.

Total Literacy Campaign (TLC)

TLC has been successful in raising the demand for education especially among women. In most of the 430 districts, women made up over 60% of adults enrolled in the programme. The classes have motivated women to fight for minimum wages and launch a crusade against prohibition. In campaign mode, the Programme actively seeks to attract women and girls to participate in the educational process. In 195 TLC districts, post literacy campaigns have begun and these address the needs of neo- literate learners. TLC is gradually being extended in the educationally backward states.

Lok Jumbish (LJ)

LJ has sharpened its strategy to mobilise and involve the whole village in the process of primary education. From amongst the villagers, potential volunteers are identified who will work towards improving education and gradually assume the role of becoming the core team. Women are encouraged to join the core team. It is ensured that there are women field personnel in every cluster (collection of villages). The field centres at the cluster level play an important role in training women's groups and providing continuing education for girls who have completed class V and are unable to go to day schools. Financial assistance for girls from weaker sections, formation of an active group within VECs for promotion of girls' education, free distribution of books, organising Kishori Manch (adolescent girls' forum) for the adjustment and empowerment of adolescent girls, are important initiatives of this project.

Non-Formal Education Programme

The NFE programme caters to the special needs of working children, girls and children in far-flung schoolless habitations. Under the programme, states are being given 60% central assistance for coeducational centres and 90% for girls' centres. The programme, at present, covers around seven million children (majority of whom are girls) in 23 states/UTs in about 279,000 centres. About 118,000 centres run under the Programme are exclusively for girls.

Working Children

Child labour has been one of the major concerns in the socioeconomic development of India. According to the 1991 Census, there were 11.28 million child labourers in the country. Promotion of education for working children as a special target group requires specific strategies and programmes.

Under the National Child Labour Projects, 1810 special schools are being run in 76 districts covering 104,400 children to impart education to children with a view to weaning them away from work. The Ministry of Labour proposes to expand this programme to cover about 2 million children by the year 2002. The department of Education will coordinate and cooperate with the Ministry of Labour in this endeavor.

Educational Development of Scheduled Castes and Scheduled Tribes

Scheduled Castes constitute 16.3% of the population and Scheduled Tribes, 8%. Overall, both the groups lag behind the general population in terms of enrolment, literacy and other indicators of progress. However, they are not homogeneous target groups. There are wide variations between SC and ST groups regionally.

The following special provision for SCs and STs have been incorporated in existing schemes of the educational programmes.

— All state governments have abolished tuition fees in government and local body school at least up to upper primary level.

— Most of the states provide assistance to students belonging to SC and ST communities for meeting other costs of education, such as text books, uniforms, stationery, schools bags and transport.

— Secondary education is free for children belonging to SCs and STs in all states and Union Territories.

— Under the Scheme of National Scholarship at secondary stage for talented children from rural areas, 13,000 scholarships are provided to SC/ST students out of the total of 43,000 scholarships annually.

— The central Institute of Indian Languages (CIIL) Mysore, prepares textbooks, primers, grammars, dictionaries, bilingual textbooks, facilitating translation from regional languages into tribal languages.

Minorities and Educational Development

Both linguistic and religious minorities deserve special consideration in expansion and promotion of elementary education. An area intensive programme for educationally backward minorities was launched in 1993 with the objectives of providing basic infrastructure and facilities in areas of concentration of educationally backward minorities which do not have adequate provision for elementary and secondary education. Under the scheme, 100% financial assistance is provided to stage governments and voluntary organisations (through state governments) for the following programmes.

— Establishment of new primary/upper primary schools and non- formal education centres where such need is felt and viability established on the basis of a school mapping exercise.
— Strengthening of educational infrastructure and physical facilities in the primary/upper primary schools.
— Opening of multi-stream residential higher secondary schools for girls where science, commerce, humanities and vocational courses are taught.

Towards Integration of the Disabled

According to POA, 1992 there are about 12.6 million differently abled children in the age group 5-18.

With an aim to place children with disabilities on par with other children, the government has chalked out a concrete programme. Under this initiative, to provide for the integrated education of the disabled children, it has been funding interventions for the integrated education of primary school children with mild to moderate disabilities.

Provision of in-service teacher training for the development of skills and competencies for early detection of disabilities, resource support for integrated education at block/district level with nongovernmental agencies, educational aids and appliances to primary school children, innovative designs for primary schools are some of the activities undertaken under this programme.

The recently enacted Disabilities Act, 1995 provides for compulsory access to school to every disabled child.

The Persons with Disabilities (Equal Opportunities, Protection of Rights and Full Participation) Act, 1995

This Act which came into force on the 1st of January, 1996, ensures

— provision of free education to children with disabilities by appropriate governments and local authorities;

— implementation of schemes and programmes for non formal education;

— research activities for designing and developing new assistive devices, teaching aids, etc.;

— setting up of teachers' training institutions to develop trained manpower for schools for children with disabilities;

— preparation of comprehensive education scheme providing for transport facilities, supply of books, etc.;

— provision of amanuensis services to students with visual handicap by the educational institutions.

4

Mid-day Meal Programme

The concept of Mid-Day Meal has a long history in India. In 1925, a MidDay Meal Programme was introduced for children belonging to poor socioeconomic status in Madras Corporation area. In 1928, Keshav Academy of Calcutta introduced compulsory Mid-Day Tiffin for school boys on payment basis at the rate of four annas per child per month.

In 1941, in parts of Kerala, the School Lunch Programme was started. in 1942, Bombay started implementing a free Mid-Day Meal Scheme. A Mid-Day Meal Scheme was introduced in Bangalore city in 1946, to provide cooked rice and yoghurt. In 1953, Uttar Pradesh Government introduced a scheme, on voluntary basis, to provide meals consisting of boiled or roasted or sprouted grams, ground-nut, puffed rice, boiled potatoes or seasonal fruits.

In the 1950s, many States came to introduce mid-day meal programmes with the assistance of different international agencies like UNICEF, FAO and WHO. International voluntary/charity organisations like Catholic Relief Service (CRS), Church World Service (CWS), CARE, USA's Meals for Million, etc, also came forward to assist in these programmes. During 1958-59, an Expanded Nutrition Programme (ENP) jointly by FAO, WHO, UNICEF and Government of India was introduced, which was subsequently expanded into Applied Nutrition Programme (ANP).

The idea of a National Mid-Day Meal Programme had been considered again and again for over a decade. In 1982, the idea of 'Food for Learning' with FAO commodity assistance was mooted. Scheduled Caste (SC) and Scheduled Tribe (ST) girls were to be covered under this programme.

In 1983, the Department of Education in the Central Government after interministerial consultations, prepared a scheme as per the guidelines of the World Food Programme (WFP). As per this, 13.6 million SC children and 10.09 ST girls in classes I-V were to be covered in 15 States and 3 Union Territories, where the enrolment of SC/ST girls was less than 79 per cent. The food material required as aid from WFP for one year was estimated to be 392,696 mts. of food grains, 19,635 mts. edible/butter oil, and 19,635 nits. of milk powder.

In monetary terms, the total annual cost of commodity assistance was $163.27 M. (Rs.1551.17 M. at an exchange rate of Rs.9.50/US V. The other cost, such as transportation, handling, cooking, etc., were to be borne by the State Governments. The proposal was circulated among States and UTs. Many States were willing to implement the programme. However, some States expressed certain difficulties. Rajasthan, for example, intimated that in case WFP assistance was withdrawn, the State would not be able to continue the programme on its own. Uttar Pradesh intimated that it would not be practicable to have mid-day meals only for SC/ST children.

A programme for Central Government assistance for mid-day meals for children in primary schools throughout the country was again considered during the year 1984-85. The broad rationale for the programme were the following:

- — Mid-day meal programme for primary schools could be construed as an antipoverty educational programme;
- — Implementation of this programme for the age-group of 6-11 may maximise enrolments and reduce school drop-out rates and this would be important from the point of view of universalisation of elementary education;
- — This would help in providing nutrition to the under-fed and under -nourished children in the rural areas; provision of meals to children in schools would also 'release foodgrains' in poor families for non-school going children; and, in effect, this would be an investment in human resource

The broad features of the programme were:

- — Coverage of primary school children in a phased manner so that by the end of the seventh Plan, 9.54 crore children could be covered; the estimated expenditure for the whole plan being Rs.4000 crore;
- — Provision of uniform nutrition for the children at 300 calories per day with 1215 grams of protein (100 grams of cereal, 10 grams of dal and 5 grams of edible oil);
- — Expenditure per child, including expenses on administration to be 60 paise;
- — Food Corporation of India to release food grains at Central Issue Prices; the value of which to be counted against Central assistance to State, estimated Central assistance for the year 1989-90 being reckoned at Rs. 623.50 crore;

— No elaborate administrative infrastructure to be built up;

— Linkage of implementation of the scheme with existing civil supplies distribution system;

— Supply of rations to be in kind and deliveries thereof be made through State/cooperative agencies;

— Central assistance to be limited to 50 per cent;

— Each State to have its own specific scheme with appropriate infrastructure and delivery systems subject to laid down parameters;

— Scheme to be implemented during the 7th Plan period in a phased manner;

— Funds to be provided, for the programme not to be construed as part of the outlay under the Head 'Education';

— Funds required for the programme to come from provisions earmarked for poverty alleviation scheme.

— While wheat and rice could be supplied through the Food Corporation of India, States would have to make their own arrangements for pulses and oil;

— States should evolve suitable logistics and make arrangements for cooks, helpers, administration, supervision and monitoring;

— Implementation of the scheme to start with ICDS blocks; monitoring mechanism evolved under ICDS to be adopted/adapted for mid-day meal scheme as well;

— Community involvement in the implementation of the scheme;

It was also recognised that the scheme had certain inherent problems such as possibilities of leakage, inadequacy of buildings, non-attendance of teachers, participation by non-school going children, abuse by those incharge, etc. It was, however, presumed that the problems would get addressed as the programme got moving. The Planning Commission prepared a set of guidelines for implementation of the scheme during the seventh Five Year Plan. However, the programme was not approved as part of the seventh Plan, nor were proposals taken up for consideration during the annual plans, apparently due to resource constraints.

The Fifth All India Educational Survey had brought out the following facts on the coverage of mid-day meals in 1986. Free mid-day meals were provided to 13.67 million or 15.91 per cent primary school students and to 7.07 million or 25.93 per cent upper primary school students. Inter-state variations ranged from nil coverage in Manipur to 46.14 per cent in Sikkim, 47.55 per cent in Tamil Nadu, 47.84 per cent in West Bengal, 53.23 per cent in Dadra and Nagar Haveli, 56.07 per cent in Tripura and 59.94 per cent in Lakshadweep at the primary level. Mid-day meals were provided in 27.9 per cent primary, 24.28 per cent upper primary, 7.20 per cent secondary and 11.82 per cent higher secondary schools. In rural areas, 28.28 per cent primary, 25.06 per cent upper primary, 7.51 per cent secondary and 11.8 per cent higher secondary schools had provision for mid-day meals as against 24.75 per cent primary, 20.91 per cent upper primary, 6.31 per cent secondary and 11.84 per cent higher secondary schools in urban areas. There were 22.6 million students who were availing of this facility at all levels of school education; of these 78.41 per cent were studying in rural schools, 40.98 per cent were girls, 20.05 per cent were Scheduled Caste Children and 12.81 per cent were Scheduled Tribe children.

In December 1988, the Department of Education formulated a proposal for covering 994 ICDS blocks with concentration of SC/ST children. It was suggested that if the Programme was to be implemented in all the ICDS blocks, (994) with concentration of tribal and scheduled caste population @ Re.1/-per child per day for primary school children, the annual expenditure would come to about Rs. 277.32 crore. The important elements of the guidelines for this scheme, which were based on thc earlier guidelines prepared by the Planning Commission, were the following:

— The scheme should cover all children in primary classes in government, government -aided and local body schools.

— Mid-day meals should be provided on all school working days.

— Ration for mid-day meals may be as follows:-

(a) Cereals -100 gms per day per child

(b) Pulses -10 " " " (Dal)

(c) Edible Oil -5 " " "

(d) Fuel

— Care assistance, if any, should be excluded.

— Cereals and, to the extent possible, pulses, edible oil and condiments should be supplied to the schools through authorised State agencies; State Governments may make use of the distribution infrastructure of Civil Supplies Corporations, cooperative agencies or other departmental outlets; Food Corporation of India would deliver stocks of wheat and rice to the State Government agencies nominated for the purpose in its depots at central issue prices.

— To the maximum extent possible, wheat should be utilised for mid-day meals, supply of rice being restricted to pre-dominantly rice eating areas. Other grains locally available could also be utilised by the States-

— States should make arrangements for appointment of cooks, helpers and supervisors. As far as possible, the cook should be a woman. The cooks and helpers should be from the same village. The State should make necessary arrangements for storage of food materials, cooking and service.

— Maximum public cooperation should be sought involving local people's representatives to oversee smooth flow of materials and service of meals.

— For the management of the scheme parallel administrative machinery should not be built up. Existing infrastructure should be used with the fullest feasible delegation of powers.

— At the District level, there should be a Supervisory Committee under the Chairmanship of the District Collector; at the State level, there should be a Committee under the Chief Secretary with members drawn from different concerned Departments. At the Central level also, there should be a Monitoring Committee with representatives from different Departments.

In 1990-91, 17 State Governments were implementing a Mid-day Meal Programme for primary school children between the age-group 6-11 years with varying degrees of coverage. Twelve States, namely, Goa, Gujarat, Kerala, Madhya Pradesh, Maharashtra, Meghalaya, Mizoram, Nagaland, Sikkim, Tamil Nadu, Tripura and Uttar Pradesh, were implementing a Mid-Day Meal Programme from out of their own resources. In three States, namely, Karnataka, Orissa and West Bengal, the programme was being implemented partially from out of their own resources and partially with assistance from CARE. Two States, namely, Andhra Pradesh and Rajasthan were running the Programme only with CARE assistance and discontinued on stoppage of the assistance.

Objectives

In the Indian context, the objective of a Mid-day Meal scheme would be two fold; (i) enhance the nutrition status of school-age children and (ii) hasten the march to universalisation of elementary education.

Nutritional Status of School Going Children

Information on the nutrition status of rural children of age group 6-11 is provided by Diet and Nutrition Surveys in rural areas conducted by National Nutrition Monitoring Bureau in the eight states of Andhra Pradesh, Gujarat, Karnataka, Kerala, Madhya Pradesh, Maharashtra, Tamil Nadu and Orissa (1990-92). Only 5.57 per cent of the children surveyed have normal nutritional status while the rest have varying degrees of malnutrition (Table 1); 12.22 per cent of the boys and 15.59 per cent of the girls suffer from severe malnutrition.

Table -1

Nutritional status of 6-11 year rural children (Criterion : Weight for age)

	Percentage of children with nutritional grades of Degree of Malnutrition			
Sex	*Severe*	*Moderate*	*Mild*	*Normal*
Boys	12.22	53.83	28.53	5.42
Girls	15.59	50.45	28.23	5.73
Pooled	13.89	52.16	28.38	5.57

The classification of nutritional status was based on normative weight for the age; children with a weight of 90 per cent and above the normative weight for the age are classified as belonging to 'normal' nutrition grade; the rest are deemed to be malnourished. A 75-90 per cent of the weight norm is classified as mild degree malnutrition, 60-75 per cent moderate degree and below 60 per cent severe degree. The dietary consumption pattern of these children was assessed using a 24 hour recall method. It was observed that the children have a deficit of the magnitude of about 628 kcal of energy and 6-7 gm protein. The energy gap constituted about 1/3rd of the daily calorie requirement. If the energy gap is bridged, the protein gap will be automatically filled. The data on the dietary intake are presented in Table 2.

Table 2. Mean protein and calorie intakes of rural children of 6-11 years age

Age (Years)	*Boys* Protein (g)	*Boys* Calories (Kcal)	*Girls* Protein (g)	*Girls* Calories (Kcal)
5-6	28.45	1102	27.86	1070
6-7	31.00	1163	29.20	1104
7-8	32.56	1252	31.45	1211
8-9	36.50	1379	36.08	1380
9-10	37.85	1458	37.55	1443
Mean Intakes	33.1	1272	32.8	1257
Mean RDI	39.5	1903	40.0	1866

Earlier studies by D. Agarwal and others confirm that malnutrition is pervasive among school children belonging to poor, rural population. These studies also bring out the prevalence of vitamin A deficiency; for instance, in Uttar Pradesh 4.1 per cent of school children had ocular signs of vitamin A deficiency, which indicates an advanced condition. According to the eminent nutrition scientist, C. Gopalan at least twenty per cent of children in rural schools at any given point of time suffer from chronic or acute infections such as otitis media, sore throat, rheumatic heart disease, etc. An annotated bibliography of the prevalence of malnutrition and parasites in developing countries brings out that 48.4 per cent school age children have chronic malnutrition, 69.4 per cent iron deficiency, 55.0 per cent iodine deficiency and 48 per cent parasites. The comparative picture of a few South Asian countries is presented in Table 3. However, care should be used when comparing among countries or among deficiencies.

Table 3. Percentage of school-age children with nutritional eficiencies and parasites various years

Country	*Chronic malnutrition(a)*	*Iron deficiency*	*Iodine deficiency*	*Parasites*
Low-income countries				
Bangladesh	71.0	74.0	-	-
Bhutan	-	-	47.0	-
Burma	-	-	70.0	86.7
China	5.0	86.9	-	2.4
India	48.4	69.4	55.0	48.0
Kampuchea	67.3	-	-	-
Democratic				
Sri Lanka	-	-	12.0	-
Lower-middle-income countries				
Indonesia	69.9	-	72.5	-
Philippines	59.4	20.6	15.1	87.7
Thailand	8.0	11.4	23.5	-
Malaysia	52.7	-	-	89.0

That the children in our schools represent a vital segment of our population is obvious. They are our valuable human resources and will contribute to the bulk of our workforce by the turn of the century. Their health, nutritional status and educational attainments will, to a considerable extent, determine the quality of our nation in the years to come.

While it is true that the pre-school age group is the most important and the most vulnerable, the children of school age represent the child population which has managed to survive the perils and hazards of infancy and early childhood and has arrived at late childhood and adolescence; many of these children still carry the scars of malnutrition and disease of their earlier years; many of them also suffer from continuing malnutrition and disease.

The relationship between scholastic performance and nutritional status of the children has also been established in some studies. Unlike the pre-school period which is associated with relatively high mortality, the great majority of even malnourished children of the school age will live to grow into adulthood, and will eventually become our future adult citizens possibly with poor physical stamina and varying degrees of functional incompetence.

In this background, measures to enhance the nutritional status of school age children are important in their own right. Several studies have explored the relationship between children's nutrition status and school indicators such as, age of enrolment, grade attainment, absenteeism, achievement tests scores, general intelligence, and performance on selected cognitive tasks, including concentration in the class rooms. Protein energy malnutrition is generally caused by a deficient diet and may be exacerbated by infection with parasites. Though there is wide variation there is a significant positive relationship between nutritional status on the one hand and mental ability and academic achievement on the other. Children who are temporarily hungry typically as a result of not eating breakfast -are generally more easily distracted in class more than those who have eaten. Three micro nutrients generally affect school performance; they are iodine, iron and vitamin A. Persistent illness that contribute to repeated absence from school, heavy parasitic loads (which contribute both to school absences and malnutrition), and hearing and vision impairment adversely affect school learning.

2.6 Annexure-II summarises the findings of Indian and international studies on the impact of nutritional interventions on enrolment, retention and achievement in schools. While it is difficult to summarise the findings of these different studies, what is evident is that school nutrition programmes do improve attendance. Whether the improvement is due to transfer of income to poor families or due to nutritional value is an academic debate that does not detract from the fact that attendance improves; further, measures to address malnutrition, deficiency of micronutritents, and hearing and vision impairment do have a tangible impact on learning achievement.

The studies also caution that the programmes should carefully be designed so that they are cost-effective and do not impinge on teaching and learning time. The studies also highlight the need to sustain nutritional support programmes once introduced; countries which have introduced school feeding programmes with external commodity support found it necessary to withdraw the programmes when food aid ceased with adverse impact on school participation.

Promotion to Universalisation of Elementary Education

Ever since independence, the country has been striving to universalise elementary education, which is a constitutional obligation. The endeavours to universalise received a fillip from the National Policy of Education

(NPE), 1986 which strongly articulated the equity and empowerment dimensions of education. It categorically stated that the new Policy would lay special emphasis on the removal of disparities, and equalisation of educational opportunities by attending to the special needs of those who have been denied equality so far. Its statement on education for women's equality is very forthright and categorical. Education is perceived to be an agent of basic change in the status of women, and playing a positive, interventionist role in the empowerment of women to neutralise the accumulated distortions of the past. World over, Universalisation of Elementary Education (UEE) is increasingly perceived as a civil right indispensable for human development, be it socioeconomic development, poverty eradication, democratic practice or good governance. Equity in education is the inevitable prelude to social equity at large.

Apart from enunciating the vision and policy postulates, the National Policy on Education (NPE), 1986 and its Programme of Action (POA), which were updated in 1992, also outline concrete strategies for universalising elementary education. These strategies include micro-planning, decentralisation of educational administration, active role for communities and Non-Governmental Organisations (NGOs), a systematic and large programme for non-formal education to meet the basic educational needs of the millions of out of school children whom the school cannot reach, improving school facilities through Operation Blackboard, improving teacher competence and motivation and laying down minimum levels of learning as an anchor to improve the content and process of education. A holistic initiative which brings together all these strategies is the District Primary Education Programme (DPEP).

By any measure, India has made great strides towards the goal of universalisation of elementary education

(UEE) since 1947. There has been significant progress in terms of spread of institutions, participation and equalisation of educational opportunities. The literacy rate has nearly trebled since Independence. Access to schooling has been substantially achieved at the primary stage with 95 per cent of the rural population having access to primary schools within a one kilometre radius. The number of primary and upper-primary schools in the country has gone up from 223 thousands in 1950-51 to 728 thousands in 1993-94.

Enrolment at the primary stage increased about five fold from 19.2 million to 108.2 million in 1993-94; the increase in the upper primary stage is far higher from 3.1 million to 39.9 million. An analysis of the enrolment data reveals that the population of children moving up from the primary to the upper primary stage has been increasing steadily, from 16.3 per cent in 1950-51 to 42.5 per cent in 1993-94. The gross enrolment ratios of children in the age group 6-11 increased from 42.6 per cent in 1950-51 to 104.5 per cent in 1993-94. Likewise, the gross enrolment of 11-14 age group increased from 12.7 per cent in 1950-51 to 67.7 per cent in 1993-94.

There is, however, a strong regional dimension to UEE. While the gross enrolment ratios (GER) at the primary stage in the country as a whole and in most of the states exceed 100 per cent, there are quite a few states where the ratio is considerably lower. These include Uttar Pradesh, Bihar, Rajasthan, Haryana, Jammu and Kashmir, and Meghalaya. At the upper primary stage these states and, in addition, Andhra Pradesh, Orissa and Sikkim have GERs lower than the national average. The literacy rates of most of these states are also lower than the national average. The problem gets more complicated as the drop-out rates, though declining, continue to be high. As per data for 1993-94, 36.32 per cent of the children who entered Class I drop out before reaching Class V and

52.80 per cent of the children drop out before reaching Class VIII. Regional disparities abound in rates of the drop-outs also.

As with any educational indicator, gender disparities are conspicuous in regard to enrolment and retention, Girls' enrolment has grown at the primary stage from 5.4 million in 1950-51 to 46.4 million in 1993-94 and at the upper primary stage from 0.5 million to 15.7 million. The rate of growth of enrolment of girls has been higher than that of boys but disparities still persist -girls still account for only 42.88 per cent of the enrolment at the primary stage and 39.34 per cent at the upper primary stage. The drop-out rates of girls at the primary as well as the upper primary stage are higher than those of boys.

Gender disparities also have a regional dimension. High female literacy states (above 50 per cent) have by and large universalised primary enrolment among girls. Even in regard to upper primary enrolments Kerala, Goa, Pondicherry and Lakshadweep are very well. In Ewes with medium female literacy status (40-50 per cent) enrolment of girls appears to be satisfactory at the primary level. The situation in low female literacy states (20-40 per cent) causes concern. These states have more than half of the country's population, with just four of them (Utter Pradesh, Bihar, Madhya Pradesh and Rajasthan) accounting for 40 per cent of the country's population.

A third dimension of UEE is the participation in the educational process by the Scheduled Castes and Scheduled Tribes. According to the 1991 census, the population of Scheduled Castes (SCs) was 138.2 million (16.33 per cent) and that of Scheduled Tribes (STs) 67.8 million (8.01 per cent) of the country's total population. Because of the affirmative policies of the government, the enrolment of SCs and STs has increased considerably at the primary stage. The participation of' SCs and STs is now more or less in proportion to their share in population at the primary level. Drop-outs, though declining over the years, are significantly large. Both SC and ST populations are not homogeneous target groups in all respects. There are wide variations between different SC and ST groups regionally. Thus SC girls in Kerala are likely to be better placed than non-SC boys in some of the more backward states and districts. Gender disparities are very conspicuous among SCs and STs also.

Though concerted efforts are being made by central and state governments, UEE is still in the distant horizon. Recent studies on trends of enrolment indicate that going by past trends UEE is likely to be achieved by 2006. It is at the upper primary level that greater efforts are needed, as the gross enrolment needed to achieve universal participation in primary education (classes IN) is likely to be achieved by 2001. The past cannot and should not necessarily be the guide for the future. The nation as a whole should put in the extra efforts needed to accelerate the trends so that we can ensure free and compulsory education of satisfactory quality to all children upto 14 years of age before we enter the twenty-first century, as envisaged in the NPE, 1986.

If we are to achieve the goal of UEE, we have to squarely address the reasons which inhibit full participation in the educational process. The 42nd round of National Sample Survey provides valuable information on the reasons for non-enrolment and dropouts.Non-availability of schooling facilities accounts for only about 10 per cent of the non-enrolled children in rural India and about 8 per cent in urban areas;the difference between sexes being very small in rural areas but somewhat larger in urban areas. Nearly 30 per cent of the children both in rural and urban India gave the reason for having never enrolled as being "not interested". About 52 per cent of the urban boys and 29 per cent of urban girls could not avail of educational services because of participation in household economic activity or other economic reasons. Attending to domestic chores restrained about one per cent boys, both in rural as well as in urban areas, from ever enrolling as students. Failure was given as the reason for discontinuation of studies by 60.3 per cent of rural and 20.3 per cent of urban dropouts. An important fact in this study was that proportion of non-enrolled children decreases with increase in per capita household income.

The 1993 survey of the National Council of Applied Economic Research (NCAER) brings out the welcome fact that since 1986 proportion of 'never-enrolled' children has come down significantly in all states. In quite a few States like Maharashtra, Gujarat and Karnataka, not to speak of Kerala and Tamil Nadu, the proportion has reached negligible levels. However, the levels are still unconscionably high in many states like Bihar, Madhya Pradesh, Uttar Pradesh, Rajasthan and Andhra Pradesh.

The strategy to reduce dropout rates has to be multipronged. The six elements of the strategy that is being tried out are: (i) creation of parental awareness and community mobilisation; (ii) utilisation of institutional mechanism created through the 73rd and 74th Constitution amendments; (iii) provision of economic incentives to help poor families defray the cost of education; (iv) convergence of services in the areas of ICDS, Primary education, primary health and creches; (v) reorganising the content and process of education including adjustments of school calendar to the local situations, improving quality and making learning child centred and enjoyable through attractive school environment and teacher motivation and training; and, lastly, (vi) implementation of the new District Primary Education Programme initiative which is essentially targetted towards low female literacy districts.

Free education, guaranteed in the Constitution, cannot be taken to mean a 'no fee' system only. Even when tuition is free, however, the direct and indirect costs can be too high to ensure enrolment and learning. A number of incentives such as supply of textbooks and uniforms are being provided by many state governments to targetted groups to help reduce the direct costs of elementary education. A properly designed nutritional support can be an additional incentive to help poor families meet expenditure incidental to effective learning and thereby can be a component of the package of economic, pedagogical and institutional measures required for universalisation of elementary education. Effective delivery of nutrition support is inconceivable without the facilitative role of the local community. It is happy augury that in pursuance of the 73rd and 74th Constitutional amendments, local communities are being empowered; particularly a large number of women have begun to play an active role in democratic governance at the grass roots. This together with other initiatives including a strong political commitment of the centre and state to universalise elementary education, the generation of demand for education through the total literacy campaigns and the decision of the government to redeem the national pledge of allocating six per cent of the national income for education have created a new ambience for universalisation of elementary education. The success of the 'Green Revolution' and development of a large scale public distribution system have also created conditions facilitative for nutrition support for education. Therefore, time is now opportune for a nutrition programme for elementary education. But we have to bear in mind that, to achieve the objectives, it is to be ensured that the incentive schemes in place are better delivered, the procedures are not cumbersome, the intended benefits reach the intended families in time and in full measure.

Through the ICDS, which is on its way to being universalised, an attempt is being made to have a broad-based nutritional Support to preschool children of poor families; nutritional support to elementary education would be a continuation of the efforts at the pre-school stage.

A programme of nutrition support to education is, by its very nature, part of a total package of poverty alleviation measures aimed at improving the general health of people. It will, therefore, not be right to look upon the expenditure on such a programme as one devolving on education budget, either of the centre or of the states. In any case, at no point of time was the outlay on nutritional support to elementary education reckoned as educational expenditure. It was the Education Commission (1964-66), more popularly called the Kothari Commission, which postulated the normative expenditure on education at six per cent of the GNP; it is this postulate which is built into the National Policy on Education, 1968 and the National Policy on Education, 1986 and which is now sought to be realised by the, end of the Ninth Plan. The calculations of the Kothari Commission do not take into account the likely expenditure on nutritional support. Hence the central or state support to nutrition at the elementary stage should be excluded from the investment that would flow from the operationalisation of the six per cent norm.

Mid-Day Meal Schemes in Operation

According to the information received from the Planning Commission, thirteen states and five union territories were administering mid-day meal programmes as of 31st December, 1994. In all 20.48 million children were covered; four states Tamil Nadu (36.13 per cent of total coverage in the country), Kerala (13.67), Gujarat (12.89) and Karnataka (6.35) together accounted for 86.35 per cent of the children covered. (Table 4)

Table 4. Mid-day meal progrmme details of statewise physical coverage as on 31st March, 1994

S.No.	States	Coverage (Figures in millions)
1.	Goa	0.007
2.	Gujarat	2.6
3.	Karnataka	1.3
4.	Kerala	2.8
5.	Madhya Pradesh	0.951
6.	Maharashtra	0.173
7.	Mizoram	0.020
8.	Nagaland	0.015
9.	Orissa	0.752
10.	Sikkim	0.039
11	Tamil Nadu	7.4
12	Tripura	0.320
13.	West Bengal	3.6
	Total (States)	19.977
	Union Territories (UTs):	
14.	Chandigarh	0.029
15.	Daman & Diu	0.007
16.	Delhi	0.365
17.	·Pondicherry	0.103
	Total (UTs)	0.504
	Grand Total: (States & UTS)	20.481

All the States and Union Territories were requested to furnish information on the mid-day meal programmes in operation as well as their views as to how the Central Government can support a phased expansion of the Mid-Day Meal programmes. Responses were received from

Bihar, Gujarat, Haryana, Jammu & Kashmir, Karnataka, Madhya Pradesh, Meghalaya, Orissa, Rajasthan, Tamil Nadu, West Bengal, Delhi and Pondicherry. The programme is not implemented in Haryana, Jammu and Kashmir, Madhya Pradesh, Meghalaya, Orissa and Rajasthan.

In Tamil Nadu, Pondicherry, Bihar and Gujarat food is prepared either in the school or its vicinity and served hot in the school while in Karnataka and Delhi pre-cooked food is served. Infact, Karnataka provides two kinds of food: a 'ready-to-eat processed energy food' and raw food in the form of soya mixed wheat powder, wheat corn, which is issued in one kg. carry-home packets every month for eight months. In Gujarat, during 1990-92, the service of cooked food was dispensed with; instead wheat at the rate of 10kg. per family was being distributed to school children belonging to poor families subject to 70 per cent attendance as certified by the school principal. Later, the state reverted to the practice of serving cooked food. West Bengal adopts a combination; bread in Calcutta and several districts and cooked food in some other districts.

In the menu for hot meal there is wide variety. 'This is as it should be. In Tamil Nadu cooked rice and sambar made of dhal, soya and vegetables, condiments and oil are provided. In addition to the regular noon-meal, one boiled egg is given once every fortnight. In Gujarat, the meal contains, wheat or joar, or bajra or maize, rice, pulses, cooking oil, vegetables and condiments. The menu is decided locally daily. In West Bengal, under the cooked food category, bulgur wheat and salad oil aye provided. In Pondicherry, the meal consists of rice, sambar and poriyal.

Bihar stands apart in the matter of mid-day meal programme. Here the beneficiaries are served 100 grams meat per child per day twice a week on Mondays and

Thursdays. The daily menu consists of wheat, dal, vegetables with condiments and cooking oil. Such a menu, of course, is costlier than the ones in other states, costing Rs. 5.40 per child per day.

There are wide variations in coverage. In Bihar the programme covers 23,800 children in 119 Charwah schools. In Karnataka 3.7 million children in all government primary schools in the state studying in primary classes are covered by the programme. In Gujarat all primary students are eligible on school working days, i.e. 200 days a year; however, as against an enrolment of 5.8 million only about 2.7 million children avail of the programme; surprisingly, the participation in the programme is about 49 per cent in the relatively less developed Northern Gujarat and Saurashtra, while it is higher, of the order of 75 per cent, in Central and Southern Gujarat. In Tamil Nadu, all students of all schools in the state from standard I to X regularly attending the school are provided the "noon-meal" round the year; the coverage is 7.4 million children. In West Bengal, eighteen districts including Calcutta is covered under the programme. The number of beneficiaries is 2.62 million under the cooked meal programme and 0.22 million under the bread propgramme. In Delhi, the programme covers 0.4 million children. In 'Pondicherry, all children in government schools studying in classes I to VIII are eligible. The present coverage is 103 thousand.

Invariably in the states where cooked food is served part-time/voluntary workers are engaged to prepare and distribute the food. In addition to nutrition programme, some states also have programme of supply of medicines with a view to improving the health of school children. From 1994, Gujarat had begun providing three types of therapeutic medicines to supplement nutrition: alpandzol (for parasitic infections); iron and vitamin A. Tamil Nadu has a separate school health programme.

In Bihar and Karnataka, the scheme is being implemented by the Education Department. In Pondicherry, Health Department is the coordinating department; in Tamil Nadu the programme is implemented by the Social Welfare Department with the strong support of Mother-Teacher Council in primary schools and Parent-Teacher Association in High schools. Cooking sheds, utensils and store rooms are provided at each noon-meal centre. The Tamil Nadu Civil Supplies Corporation is vested with the responsibility of delivery to the noon-meal centre of articles supplied through public distribution system. As a prestigious programme of the State Government, monitoring and supervision are fairly intense. In Gujarat the scheme is implemented in urban areas by the Municipal bodies and in rural areas under the supervision of the District Collector with the involvement of revenue and education officials.

In Tamil Nadu, noon-meal is provided throughout the year, in other states it is limited to the school working days. In Tamil Nadu the food provided is equivalent to about 500 -600 calories depending on the age-group while in Gujarat it is stated to be of 450 calories.

Depending on the menu offered, there is wide variation in the cost per unit also, ranging from Re.1 in West Bengal to Rs.5.40 in Bihar. We observe that Tamil Nadu and Gujarat have been able to provide calorie input of 450-600 within a unit cost of around Re. 1.50. This could be taken as a norm for unit cost.

The Rajasthan Government had expressed the view, which was also articulated by the State Education Secretary who met the Committee on May 17, 1995 that the State Government has reservations on the utility of mid-day meal programme and that the expenditure on such a programme is better invested on programmes having a direct bearing on UEE such as supply of uniforms to girls and free textbooks. While the State

Government may go by what the Government of India decides it would prefer distribution of foodgrains with the freedom to the State Government to use the proceeds of the foodgrains to an educational scheme approved by the Government of India. The Committee does not share this view.

Scope of School Lunch Programmes

Conceptually one can envisage a wide range of possibilities: at the one end is a comprehensive programme covering all children in elementary schools with provisions of not only nutritious hot mid-day meal but also universal school based health coverage. In fact, there is a respectable point of view, advocated by Dr. C. Gopalan, that to yield really durable results the Mid-Day Meal Programme has to go hand in hand with, and be an integral part of a well-organised School Health Service. As per his assessment at least 30 per cent of children in rural schools at any given point of time are suffering from chronic or acute infections such as obitis media, sore throat, and rheumatic heart diseases. In the face of such infactions, school meals cannot make as significant an impact on health and nutritious status as they otherwise would. It is only if school meal is part of a school health service that the impact would be gratifying. To quote Dr. C. Gopalan:

> The midday meal Programme in schools, which generated a great deal of enthusiasm some years ago, has also by and large, proved to be no shining success, apart from a few exceptions. Some recent evaluation studies have indicated positive benefits of midday meal programme but, by and large, the results in other situations have not been apparently convincing enough to generate continuing enthusiasm. The reason for this again has been that midday meal programmes have been conceived of and implemented as isolated programmes, without any serious attempt to integrate

them as an element of comprehensive school health service.

Many midday meal programmes were undertaken merely because free foreign food doles were available; and it was the mechanics of the feeding operation and the disposal of the food that claimed the main attention. A school lunch programme in a school which has no access to safe water supply, and in which a high proportion of children suffer from chronic infections like septic tonsils or middle-ear disease, cannot be expected to work wonders. Indeed it will be a waste of precious resources. On the other hand, a purposeful and well monitored midday meal programme adapted to suit the local needs, based on locally available food ingredients, integrated with a school health programme and used as a means of nutrition education of the 'school community' can prove rewarding.

Therapeutic programme: Indeed, where resources are limited, a midday meal programme, instead of being conducted as a blanket welfare operation, can even be undertaken as a 'therapeutic' programme, specifically directed to school children identified in the course of medical inspection as suffering from moderate or severe malnutrition, and limited in each case to the duration considered necessary on medical grounds and till the family can be educated and persuaded to improve the child's diet; such a programme may be based on ready-to-eat nutritious snacks prepared in village cooperatives from locally available foods.

In some situations, in rural areas such dietary supplementation may be found necessary only in certain seasons of the year -such as the preharvest season when there is widespread under-employment among parents and acute poverty. There is a case of modifying and restructuring our school lunch programmes on these and other lines but not for totally abandoning them.

Less comprehensive in scope is the supply of hot mid-day meal programme with more limited health coverage by way of supply of vitamins, iron, etc. As one proceeds down the continuum there are options like supply of hot cooked food sans health coverage, of pre-cooked food, and of food grains.

Ideally the more comprehensive the programme, the better it is; choice, however, is constrained by the availability of resources, financial as well as organisational. Organisational requirements are likely to be more exacting than financial resources; therefore phasing and gradual step up of the programme are warranted by the criteria of sustainability and cost-effectiveness. It would be necessary to provide for variations among states; states which have been implementing nutrition support to education with a certain degree of success can move with ease to more comprehensive options while others may like to move by stages.

Whatever might be the mode of delivery of nutrition support per se, we would commend strong linkages between primary education and the primary health centre network so that the basic health care needs of children are catered to. We would like nutrition support to be perceived as part of a comprehensive package bringing together health, nutrition, early childhood care and primary education.

The synergies that can be derived by coordinated implementation of related programmes have been established by many studies including the Project Nutrition, Health Education and Environmental Sanitation (NHEES) conducted by NCERT in collaboration with SCERTs. The project was tried out in select blocks in fifteen states and union territories over the period 1975-89. Common micro-nutrient deficiencies, chronic or acute infections, visual and speech impediments of school children need to be identified and remedied by linkages between the school and primary health care system. We take note of the fact that many states have taken initiatives in this regard. To illustrate, the programme as implemented in Gujarat, provides for supply of medicines, vitamin A and iron; the Health Department of Tamil Nadu has mounted a strong school health programme separately. Likewise a school health project is in implementation in Andhra Pradesh with the assistance of the Overseas Development Agency, United Kingdom. A school health programme is being tried out on a pilot basis in ten districts covered by the Uttar Pradesh Basic Education Project funded by the World Bank.

The Ministry of Human Resource Development has been attempting to promote convergence, the circulars issued by Department of Women and Child Development and by the Department of Education are at Annexure IV. Further, the Planning Commission has formulated guidelines and commended them to the States (also given in Annexure IV). We would strongly commend them to the States for speedy and effective implementation for it is only through convergence that we can realise the synergies of related programmes only through convergence can the country move, fast towards the goal of comprehensive child care.

Mode pf Delivery

The three basic choices are: (1) supply of hot meal, (ii) pre-cooked food and (iii) food grains. Each of these have their merits and demerits which need to be taken note of while finally deciding on the specifics of the programme.

The hot meal is likely to be the most satisfying to the rural communities and is likely to have best outcomes if the food is hygienically prepared based on sound nutritional principles and if the exacting requirements of logistics, operations and monitoring are met continuously without let or hindrance. From the nutritional angle the endeavour should be to bridge the average nutritional gap of about 600 cal. through a balanced diet of cereals, pulses, oil and vegetables. The cereal component could be of the order of 100 gms/day, or roughly, 60-70 per cent of the calorie deficit to be provided. Proposals were mooted from time to time for limited coverage to children of disadvantaged communities. However, this is not a viable option. One cannot and should not discriminate among children in the distribution of cooked food; universal provision of food to all the students can be a potent solvent of social barriers and inhibitions. If resources are a constraint, selectivity has to be introduced by restricting the number of schools to be covered; there can be additional selectivity by limiting the coverage to a few classes, say classes I-V (primary), instead of classes I-VIII (upper primary); however, all children in the classes selected for coverage should be provided the hot cooked meal.

But a logical consequence of this approach is that the programme does not target the poor; the question therefore arises whether there is an alternative mode of delivery which enables the resources to be directed to poor children who are likely to have lower nutritional status and whose families may require incentives to defray the associated costs of education; it is here that the 'Food for Education' makes the debut. Particularly in states with lower enrolment ratios and higher drop-out rates and which are further down on the road to UEE targetting towards poorer families has greater merit.

Pro-rata, the supply of cereal/child under Food For Education would have to be higher than the hot meal variant. It is reasonable to expect that only a part of the food grains supplied to the family would be available to the school going children; while this is not desirable from the nutritional point of view, it has the incidental merit of being a stronger economic incentive to the family to send the child to school. Further, a higher scale of foodgrain supply is warranted by the fact that the foodgrains at 100 gm/day would cover only 60-70 per cent of the calorific gap that is proposed to be covered. Assuming that the child would receive only 50 per cent of the foodgrains supplied to the families and assuming that the foodgrain so devolving on the child would be 70 per cent of the calorific gap a supply of foodgrains 5 kg/child to the family for ten months would be equivalent to the supply of 100 gms/day/child for 200 school days under the hot food variant. We would recommend this as the norm for the Food For Education variant.

While the supply of hot food would be linked with the actual attendance of the child, surrogate norms would have to be devised for the Food For Education variant. A minimum attendance of 80 per cent could be taken as the eligibility criterion. We considered the possibility of limiting the number of children per family who could be covered under Food For Education variant so that small family norm is promoted. While such a linkage has plausible merit, it is beset with operational problems and is also inconsistent with the normative objective itself. The eligibility criterion becomes more complex; if a family has more than two children at school, eligibility would have been linked with the 80 per cent attendance of atleast two school children in the family. Not only is this cumbersome to implement this criterion may militate against the small family norm itself. Such an eligibility criterion may discriminate against female participation. There is ample empirical evidence linking low birth rates with higher level of nutrition and longer years of schooling among girls; the small family norm is therefore likely to be better served by ensuing that every child goes to school and completes the primary and upper primary cycle of eight years. Therefore, we would suggest that no ceiling on number of children for benefits under the scheme need be prescribed.

The choice among the two alternatives so far discussed is also linked with organisational resources required to deliver the programme. A hot mid-day meal scheme is inevitably more exacting in its requirement of organisation, logistics and monitoring. Common to both options is the essentiality of an effective public distribution system whereby adequate quantities of foodgrains regularly reach the village for distribution to the school or to the family. In addition to this common requirement, the hot food variant calls for the infrastructure and manpower to procure the provisions other than the foodgrains, store them, cook the food in hygienic conditions and serve them. Given the paramount objective of ensuring that the teaching and learning time is not curtailed and given the understandable reluctance of teachers not to be held responsible for organising the programme it would be necessary to create additional facilities and manpower. States like Gujarat and Tamil Nadu have found it necessary to appoint part-time or volunteer women like, organiser, cook and helper. However, there have been problems of unionisation and demands for regular service and comparable wages. If the programme is to operate on a large scale on a sustained basis it would be necessary to explore alternatives to creation of large cadres of part-time workers or volunteers. Many possibilities exist; they have to be explored, e.g. the use of Non-Governmental Organisations(NGOs), DWACRA groups, linkages with ICDS and so on. The creation of facilities, effective and viable in the long run, has to be an essential condition for introduction of the hot-food variant. Large scale creation of governmental cadres, whatever be their nature, is undesirable.

With any of the variant, constant vigilance is necessary to prevent leakages and to ensure that the intended benefits reach the intended beneficiaries. Though less demanding on logistics the Food For Education variant calls for more rigorous mechanism for maintaining fidelity in the determination of entitlement. An odd spot check of attendance is not likely to be effective as entitlement is related to average attendance rather than attendance on the day of check. Hence, Food For Education is more demanding in its reliance on the local communities for preventing leakages. Therefore, with any variant Panchayat Bodies, Village Education Committees, Mother/Parent Teachers Councils, and Mahila Samakhya representatives have a crucial role in facilitating and overseeing the programme.

The uncompromising logistical demands of hot meal variant can be obviated by the delivery of pre-cooked food. Quite a few alternatives are in operation in some states, e.g., supply of bread in Calcutta, of bread/bun/ fried grams in Delhi, processed food in Karnataka, etc. This option is particularly viable in urban areas with well developed chains of manufacturers and suppliers. However, it is a moot point how far this is a viable option in remote areas where the continuous supply, of processed food may not be viable and may not necessarily suit the tastes of children. Further the cost/ calorie is likely to be higher as the value added in manufacture would be higher than the cost of conventional cooking and has to be provided for.

Thus, to sum up, each variant has its merits and demerits; the adaptability is contextual. As organisational arrangements fall in place, and resources expand it may be possible to move toward universal coverage of all school children with hot meal or a combination of hot meal and processed food. In the interim, it would be desirable to provide flexibility to the state governments giving them an option to choose among the variants or opt for a combination of variants. It is conceivable that in the same state, in the metropolitan areas precooked food is supplied, hot food in blocks where favourable conditions can be created and food for education elsewhere. However, from the operational point of view only one mode of delivery should be chosen for all the schools in a block and the choice should not vary during the year.

Selectivity By Stage

In the face of resources and operational requirement constraints, an additional dimension of selectivity is provided by stages of elementary education, viz., primary and upper primary education. In most states there are schools which exclusively impart primary education. It should, however, be noted that the number of years covered by primary education varies -it could be 4 or 5 years. Therefore, it is possible to have the programme limited to primary schools; even coverage of primary classes within an upper primary school through a hot food is not as invidious a discrimination as limiting the coverage in a given class. However, from the point of view of UEE, coverage of upper primary classes is essential; gross enrolment ratios are considerably lower and drop-out rates higher at the upper primary stage; it is enhanced participation at the upper primary stage that would determine the time by when elementary education is universalised. Given our objective to accelerate these trends coverage of upper primary classes has great educational merit. Considering that infrastructure would be in place, extention of coverage to upper primary classes should pose no extra effort. We would, however, suggest that from operational point of view nutrition support to education be extented to all government, local body and aided schools which account for more than 96 per cent of primary schools in the country. We do not commend coverage of other schools as most of them are either unrecognised or high fee charging schools catering to the better off families. Coverage of unrecognised schools may generate litigation as management of such schools may contend that coverage tantamounts to recognition by State Government.

Involvement of Local Community

It is now axiomatic that development must be socially just, economically viable and environmentally benign and, for that purpose, people have to be placed at the centre of planning and implementation. Education, as perceived by the National Policy on Education, 1986 is an instrument for empowerment of people. Involvement of local community, village panchayat and non-governmental organisations is critical for the successful implementation of a programme of nutrition support to education. It is now well established that the process of development can be accelerated only by promoting the participation of people and the community in a perspective that includes designing and implementation of such activities. Developing on this theme, the Programme of Action, 1992 states unequivocally that the successful implementation of programmes like elementary education including non-formal education, early childhood care and education, adult education, education of the disabled, etc., will require people's involvement at the grass roots level and participation of voluntary agencies and social activist groups on a much larger scale. The Total Literacy Campaigns, with their unique social mobilisation of community and non-governmental organisations and partnership between government, NGOs, teachers and others have demonstrated how governmental efforts can be effectively supplemented and through people's participation. The one message that comes out loud and clear from these campaigns is that social welfare, including educational goals, cannot be achieved without the enlistment of non-governmental efforts.

In a programme like nutrition support for education multiplicity of functionaries and agencies are involved. It is only the local communities that can ensure that multiple functionaries act together and synergies are derived by the convergence of multiple but related schemes to achieve the objectives of the programme. The 73rd and 74th Constitution amendments have paved the way for enhanced participation of local community in education, health and other related programmes.

The Report of the CABE (Central Advisory Board of Education) Committee on Decentralised Management of Education indicates how educational structures should be set up at the district, block/taluk levels in pursuance of these Constitution amendments. It has also suggested ways for mobilising community participation in the educational process so that power devolves on the people in the true spirit of the amendments. We would suggest that state governments may keep in view the recommendations of the CABE committee while formulating scheme for nutrition support to education.

A major aspect of the decentralised management of education as envisaged in the Panchayati Raj Act is the formation of Village Education Committees which would be responsible for the administration of education programmes at the village level. The main responsibilities of the VECs would lie in operationalisation of micro-level planning in school mapping in the village through systematic house to house surveys and periodic discussions with parents. Ensuring participation in primary education of every child of every family would be one of the prime aims of the VECs. The programme of nutrition support to education being one of the measures to induce attendance in elementary schools, the responsibility for proper implementation could be entrusted to the VECs wherever they have been set up. The VECs should also be able to ensure that the programme is implemented in the fight manner and the intended benefits reach the intended beneficiaries, whether it is the hot meal variant or the Food for Education variant. Particularly in the Food for Education variant, the VEC can ensure that it is the really deserving who are covered by the programme.

Apart from the VEC, the Village Pachayat and the Panchayat Samiti should also be actively involved in the programme, They can play a very effective role in the supervision of the arrangements for the hot meal variant and, in the case of the Food for Education variant, in its distribution. We would strongly urge the active involvement of the Women Panchas in the programme.

We have elsewhere referred to the laudable role the Mother -Teacher Associations are playing in the implementation of the Tamil Nadu Noon Meal programme. The Mother/Parent Teacher Associations and groups like the DAWCRA can effectively supervise the functioning of the hot meal programme in the schools to ensure that the food is prepared and served to the children in hygienic conditions, that the food is to the taste of the children, that there is enough variety in the menu to avoid monotony in the fare served. Their presence at the time of service should also help in orderly distribution and in guaranteeing that no child is discriminated against in the matter of quantity of food served. It is natural to expect that an actively involved Association would chip in with additionalities in the food served. Further, the presence of at least some mothers at the meal time will create a homely atmosphere for the children.

The non-governmental organisations, including the consumer groups, apart from contributing to the programme, can serve as watchdogs against misappropriation and misutilisation. Constant vigilance is the only guarantor of effective functioning of any welfare programme. The role of NGOs is particularly heightened in the Food for Education variant. Bogus enrolment figures, inclusion of undeserving families in the list of beneficiaries, non-issue of the allotted quantity of food grains to the beneficiaries, poor quality of the food grains issued, etc., are the areas, which require to be closely watched.

The NGOs, through occasional visits to the schools and the PDS shops can detect malpractices and bring them to the notice of the authorities expeditiously. The kind of Vigilance Committees envisaged under the Revamped Public Distribution System which comprise card holders (i.e., beneficiaries), consumer organisations and women's groups to oversee working of Fair Price Shops, supply of essential commodities to the beneficiaries and to detect bogus ration cards is an emulative step for involvement of community and nongovernmental organisations in the nutrition support for education programme. They can also play a very effective role in creating parental awareness and thus enhancing enrolment and retention in schools.

5

Planning of Adult Education

India's multiplicity of institutions have ensured a smooth flow of knowledge from one generation to another. The quest for learning, evident in the Vedas, Upanishadas, Jataks and other mythological texts was further reinforced at ancient centres of learning like Nalanda, Takshila and Vikramshila. Alongside flourished several forms of folk culture and tradition like kathas, kirtans, jatras, palas, daskathas and other forms of traditional performing and plastic arts.

Over the years, the scenario has undergone a sea-change. The days of 'Sruti' are long over. Tremendous modernisation both in the means of communication as well as the content have imparted a new dimension to the entire process. Phenomenal information explosion and diversification in the means of communication have ensured dissemination of news relating to development and growth is not confined to a particular region.

While this is particularly evident in the more developed parts of the world, it is not so in the developing ones, where large cross-sections continue to be illiterate. With hardly any access to information, modernisation and communication and virtually no access to the irreducible minimum survival tools, they remain helpless victims of poverty, deprivation and exploitation. The benefits of plans and programmes do not percolate to them and they remain cut-off from the mainstream.

Literacy an important tool for communication, learning and information, is a virtual precondition for an individual's evolution and national development. Research studies on human cognitive development have established that literacy enhances the critical faculties and enables to reflect on the existential reality in which they have been placed. It promotes objectivity, capacity for clear perception, thought, logical and coherent analysis. It promotes a sense of history and helps combine individuality with universalisation. In this sense, literacy can be regarded as an inalienable fundamental right.

Post-independence India inherited a system of education which was characterised by large scale inter and intra-regional imbalances. The system educated a select few, leaving a wide gap between the educated and the illiterate. The country's literacy rate in 1947 was only 14 per cent and female literacy was abysmally low at 8 per cent. Only one child out of three had an opportunity for enrolment in primary schools. Educational inequality was aggravated by economic inequality, gender disparity and rigid social stratifications.

Eradication of illiteracy has been one of the major national concerns of the Government of India since Independence. The need for a literate population and universal education for all children in the age group 6- 14 was recognised as a crucial input for nation building and was given due consideration in the Constitution as well as in the successive five-year plans. A number of significant programmes have been taken up since Independence to eradicate illiteracy among adults. Some of the important programmes have included:

(i) *Social Education:* The main elements were literacy, extension, general education, leadership training and social consciousness. The programme was implemented in the First Five-Year Plan (1951-56).

(ii) *Gram Shikshan Mohim:* Movement for literacy in the rural areas was started in 1959 in Satara district of Maharashtra, and was later extended to other parts of the state. The programme aimed at imparting basic literacy skills within a period of about four months and by 1963, it spread to all the districts of the state. The programme, however, suffered from a lack of systematic follow-up and consequently, relapse to illiteracy was massive.

(iii) *Farmers' Functional Literacy Project:* Started in 1967-68 as an inter-ministerial project for farmers' training and functional literacy, the project aimed at popularisation of highyielding varieties of seeds through the process of adult education. The programme was confined to 144 districts of the country where nearly 8,640 classes were organised for about 2.6 lakh adults.

(iv) *Non-formal Education:* In the beginning of the Fifth Plan, a programme of non-formal education for 15-25 age-group was launched. Although the scope, content and objective of the non-formal project was clearly spelt out, its understanding in the field was very limited and the programmes actually organised indistinguishable from the conventional literacy programmes.

(v) *Polyvalent Adult Education Centres:* Workers' Social Education Institutes and Polyvalent Adult Education Centres were reviewed by a group in 1977, which recommended adoption of Polyvalent Adult Education Centres in the adult education programme for workers in urban areas. In pursuance of this decision, Shramik Vidyapeeths were set up in the states.

(vi) *Education Commission (1964-66):* The appointment of the Education Commission (1964-66) was a significant event in the history of education in India. Among several measures, it recommended that high priority be accorded to ending illiteracy. It urged that adult education be promoted both through "selective" as well as "mass approach" and stressed on the active involvement of teachers and students and the wider use of the media for the literacy programme."

The Education Commission also stated that in the world of science and technology, the main objective should be to relate it to life, needs and aspirations of the people so as to make it an instrument of socioeconomic and political change.

(vii) *Functional Literacy for Adult Women (FLAW):* The scheme of Functional Literacy for Adult Women (FLAW) was started in 1975-76 in the experimental ICDS project areas. It was gradually expanded alongwith the expansion of ICDS upto the year 1981-82.

Till then, 300 ICDS projects were approved. Sanctions were also given for FLAW scheme in these project areas. However, the Planning Commission decided to stop the expansion of FLAW scheme in ICDS project areas mainly due to a constraint of resources.

The aim of the FLAW scheme was to enable illiterate adult women to acquire functional skills along with literacy, to promote better awareness of health, hygiene, child-care practices and to bring about attitudinal changes. The target age group was 15-45, with greater attention to those in the 15-35 age group.

(viii) *National Adult Education Programme (NAEP):* The first nation-wide attempt at eradication of illiteracy was made through the National Adult Education Programme launched on October 2, 1978. It was a massive programme which aimed at educating 100 million non- literate adults in the age group of 15-35 years within a time frame of five years.

The objectives of the National Adult Education Programme were not merely to impart literacy in the conventional sense, but also to provide learners with functional awareness which were conceived as three integral components of the skills of reading, writing and arithmetic. Functionality implied the ability to utilise and apply the skills acquired with a view to promote efficiency of the neo-literate. The social awareness component aimed at knowing, understanding and taking action on issues which affect the individual community and society.

ix) *Rural Functional Literacy Project (RFLP):* This was a major centrally sponsored scheme started in 1978 for rural areas. The erstwhile 144 Farmers' Functional Literacy Projects and 60 Non-formal Education Projects were merged into it. Further, projects were added and the number of projects throughout the country in 1987 were 513, each having upto a maximum number of 300 adult education centres and each centre having 25-30 learners.

(x) *State Adult Education Programme (SAEP):* The states also similarly took up centre based projects under the state plan funds on the lines of RFLPs.

(xi) *Adult Education through Voluntary Agencies:* To ensure greater participation of voluntary agencies, the Central Scheme of Assistance to Voluntary Agencies was revived in April 1982. Under this scheme, registered societies were sanctioned Centre-based projects for functional literacy and post-literacy, where they were allowed to run projects in a compact area.

Review of the National Adult Education Programme

Intended to be a mass programme, the National Adult Education Programme (NAEP), however, remained a traditional centre-based programme, which was also honorarium based, hierarchical and government-funded and government controlled. As against the target of 100 million, a total of 44.22 million learners were enrolled in adult education centres in different years upto March 1988. On the basis of sample evaluation studies, it has been estimated that only about 45 per cent of the enrolled learners attained literacy. Thus, the level of achievement of this programme in relation to the target set for it was only about 20 per cent. The centre-based programme was reviewed and evaluated by several institutes of social science research and later, the Government of India also appointed a review committee headed by Prof. DS Kothari to assess the strengths and weaknesses of the programme. The strengths and weaknesses of the NAEP as revealed through various evaluation studies are summarised below:

Strengths

— Women's motivation and participation had been high;

— Coverage of weaker sections of the society (SCs and STs) was higher than the target;

— The project approach to management adopted for adult education programme is feasible;

— The quality of teaching-learning materials prepared

by the National Resource Centre and the State Resource Centres was found to be positive;

Weaknesses

— Quality of training of the functionaries was poor;
— The learning environment in the adult education centres was poor;
— Mass media did not provide appreciable support;
— Voluntary agencies did not receive willing co-operation from State Governments. The existing procedures for their involvement were discouraging.
— There was no linkage between basic literacy, post-literacy, follow-up and continuing education, resulting in the relapse of large number of neo-literates into illiteracy;
— Achievement levels of literacy were below the desired level;
— Training of adult education functionaries at all levels lacked participatory and communicative techniques;

Literacy Rate

Accomplishments since Independence in 1947 in terms of literacy, spread of institutions, participation and equalisation of educational opportunities have been quite significant. There has been phenomenal increase in the number of educational institutions, faculties, in teachers and students. The number of teachers has gone up five-fold and the number of schools three fold. Literacy rate has nearly trebled. The decennial census, 1991, saw India across the 50 per cent mark, achieving the literacy rate of 52.21 per cent. The table below is an indication as to how the literacy rate has increased over the four decades since 1951:

Literacy Rate - India: 1951-1991

Year	Persons	Male	Female
1951	18.33	27.16	8.86
1961	28.30	40.39	15.33
1971	34.45	45.95	21.97
1981	43.57	56.38	29.76
	(41.43)	(53.46)	(28.47)
1991	52.21	64.13	39.23

Quite apart from the rates themselves, it would be relevant to briefly consider the absolute figures of literates and illiterates. During the last four decades, population of the country has been increasing at the exponential growth rate of more than 2 per cent per annum. While the expanded educational facilities pushed up the number of literates in the country it has not been able to keep pace with the increasing population. The number of illiterates has simultaneously increased though at a declining rate of growth. In absolute terms, while the number of literates has increased from about 60 million in 1951 to about 359 million in 1991, the number of illiterates has increased from about 300 million in 1951 to about 328 million in 1991. The statement below illustrates the point:

Number of Literates and Illiterates - India: 1951-91

Year	Total Population	Age group	Illiterates (in million)	Literates
1951	361.09	-	300.09	60.19
1961	439.23	5+	267.32	105.52
1971	548.16	5+	307.19	161.41
1981	683.30	7+	305.31	235.73
1991	846.30	7+	328.88	359.28

It would also be noticed from the above table that the number of literates has exceeded the number of illiterates for the first time in 1991 thereby taking the literacy rate above 50 percent landmark. Gender disparity in literacy is a historical phenomenon. In 1901, while the literacy rate for males was 9.83 per cent, it was only 0.60 per cent in the case of females.

The above table indicates that large disparity still continues in the male/female literacy situation. While about two-third of the males in the country were literate in 1991, the landmark of 50 per cent is still far beyond the rate of females. The difference between the male and female literacy rate has been of the order of about 25 percentage points during the last three decades. However, there is a silver lining. While the literacy rate among males has increased by 7.70 percentage points during the decade 1981-1991, corresponding increase in case of females is 9.34 percentage points.

There is a large urban-rural differential in literacy rates. This differential is of the order of about 30 percentage points and has continued to remain so over the last several decades as may be seen from the table below:

While about 3/4 of the urban population is literate, literacy rate in rural areas is yet much below the 50 percent mark. Literacy rate for females in rural areas is still lower, being only 30.62. When it is compared with the literacy rate of 81.09 per cent for urban male population, the gender and rural/ urban disparities become glaringly evident.

Literacy rate at the national level reveals only a part of the story of disparities in literacy situation in the country. Literacy rates among the States/UTs range from 89.81 per cent in Kerala to 38.48 per cent in Bihar. Difference between the highest and the lowest literacy rate among states/UTs is of the order of 51.33 percentage points which is even higher than the literacy rate-in Bihar. It is observed that 22 States/UTs have literacy rate higher than the national average. Nine states and union territories besides Jammu & Kashmir where 1991 census was not held are having literacy rate below the national average. On the basis of literacy rate, State/UTs can be grouped as under:

— Below 50 % - Bihar (38.48), Rajasthan, Dadra & Nagar Haveli, Arunachal Pradesh, Uttar Pradesh, Andhra Pradesh, Madhya Pradesh, Orissa, Meghalaya (49.10) and (Jammu & Kashmir).

— 50 % to 60 % - Assam (52.89), Haryana, Karnataka, Sikkim, West Bengal, Punjab, Manipur (59.89).

— 60 % to 70 % - Tripura (60.44), Gujarat, Nagaland, Himachal Pradesh, Maharashtra (64.87).

— 70 % to 80 % - Daman & Diu (71.20), A&N Islands, Pondicherry, Delhi, Goa, Chandigarh (77.81).

— 80 % and above - Lakshadweep (81.78), Mizoram, Kerala (89.81).

While Lakshadweep, Mizoram and Kerala are having literacy rate of above 80 per cent, Bihar and Rajasthan are still below 40 per cent.

In terms of the size of illiteracy, seven states of India, viz. Uttar Pradesh, Bihar, Madhya Pradesh, Rajasthan, Andhra Pradesh, West Bengal and Maharashtra have more than 20 million illiterates each and account for more than 70 per cent of the illiterate population of the country.

It is evident from the above analysis of literacy scenario in India that in spite of substantial expansion of infrastructural facilities and a large spatial spread of primary and upper primary institutions, the goal of yet been achieved. While the number providing basic education to all has not of literates of all ages has increased sixfold between 1951 to 1991, the absolute number of illiterates has also increased. India today has the dubious distinction of having the largest number of illiterates in the world. Of the total estimated 900 million illiterates in the world, around one-third reside in India alone. The two factors which primarily contribute to increase in the number of illiterates, are-

(a) rapid rate of growth of population, and

(b) failure of universalisation of elementary education characterised by low enrolment (particularly of girls), high dropout and low retention.

The above two factors in a sense are also inter- related in as much as larger the population, lesser are the resources for education and educational infrastructure including primary school buildings, libraries, laboratories, teachers' training and research. Larger the size of the family, lesser will be the children to schools and greater the availability of resources for sending propensity to retain them for odd household jobs due to sheet economic compulsions.

The problem of illiteracy is further aggravated by social constraints.

A two-pronged approach of universalisation of elementary education and universal adult literacy has been adopted for achieving total literacy. The National Policy on Education has given an unqualified priority to the following three programmes for eradication of illiteracy, particularly among women:-

a. Universalisation of elementary education and universal retention of children upto 14 years of age.

b. A systematic programme of non formal education in the educationally backward states.

c. The National Literacy Mission which aims at making 100 million adults literate by 1997.

The major thrust of these programmes is on promotion of literacy among women, members belonging to Scheduled Castes and Scheduled Tribes particularly in the rural areas.

National Literacy Mission

National Literacy Mission has been conceptualised and built on an objective assessment of the strengths and weaknesses of the earlier programmes emanating from the evaluation study reports mentioned earlier. The creation of a mission for literacy represents a national political commitment on the need to harness social forces and channelise the energies of people towards meeting the ultimate objective of effecting a qualitative change in their own lives. Conceptually, the mission focus' on:

— a new sense of urgency, seriousness and emphasis with fixed goals, clear time-frame and age-specific target groups;

— firm belief that adults can be made literate according to certain predetermined norms within a stipulated time limit (200 hours) and that it is not too late to learn;

— emphasis on the close nexus between literacy of adult parents and enrolment of school going children, on the one hand, and literacy and infant mortality, immunisation and child care on the other;

— a special mission which believes that literacy is not the concern of one ministry or department or agency but is the concern of the entire nation and all sections of society;

— emphasis on institutionalisation of post-literacy and continuing education in a big way;

— a technology mission also in the sense that besides emphasis on improvement of teaching/learning environment, it lays stress on improvement in the content and process of teaching-learning on a continuing basis;

— envisages creation of an effective mission management system to ensure achievement of the mission objectives with in a broad framework of flexibility, delegation, decentralisation and accountability;

— emphasis not on mere enrolment of learners but on attainment of certain predetermined norms and parameters of literacy, numeracy, functionality and awareness.

NLM Objective

In quantitative terms, the mission seeks to impart functional literacy to 100 million illiterate persons in 15-35 age group by the close of 1997.

In qualitative terms, functional literacy implies:

— Self-reliance in 3R's.

— Participation in the development process.

— Skill improvement to improve economic status and general well-being.

— Imbibing values of national integration, conservation of environment, women's equality and observance of small family norms etc.

The NLM seeks to achieve these objectives through the following:

(i) by creating an environment conducive to teaching-learning process, provision of good and relevant teachinglearning materials and facilitating teaching-learning by good training, media and communication;

(ii) by improving the pace of learning, and injecting confidence among the learners about their potential to learn and that the process is not drudgery;

(iii) by integrating basic literacy with post-literacy and continuing education; and

(iv) by developing the quality of human resource at all levels such as instructor, supervisor, project officer etc. through orientation and training.

NLM has defined the desired level of competencies in the 3R's as follows:

Reading

— Reading aloud, with normal accent, and at a speed of 30 words a minute, a simple passage on a topic of interest to the learner.

— Silent reading at 35 words a minute, of small paragraphs in simple language.

— Reading with understanding the road signs, posters, simple instructions, and newspapers/ broadsheets designed for neoliterates.

— Ability to follow simple written passages relating to one's working and living environment.

Writing

— Copying, with understanding, at 7 words a minute.

— Taking dictation at 5 words a minute.

— Writing with proper spacing and alignment.

— Writing independently, short letters and applications, and filling in forms of day-to-day use to the learner.

Numeracy

— Reading and writing numerals 1-100.

— Doing simple calculations (without fraction) involving addition and subtraction upto 3 digits, and multiplication and division by 2 digits.

— Working knowledge of metric units weights, measures, currency, distance, area and unit of time.

— Broad idea of proportion and interest (not involving fractions) and their use in practical situations.

Content of Learning

All adults are not uniformly endowed. They do not also learn at a uniform pace. Their ingenuity for learning, receptivity and retentivity are varied. Research has also established that adult learners are motivated to learn better if:

— the duration of learning is neither too long nor too short;

— the content of the materials is in conformity with the learners' needs;

— the learners are able to perceive the progress of learning from stage to stage.

Keeping this basic pedagogical constraint in view, a new technique of learning has been formulated and adopted by the National Literacy Mission. It is known as 'Improved Pace and Content of Learning (IPCL)', its characteristics are as indicated below:-

— There are three sets of primers, each primer being an improvement on the other in terms of progression.

— Each primer is an integrated one in the sense that it combines workbook, exercise book, tools of evaluation of learning outcome, certification, etc.

— The primers are prepared through workshops involving creative thinkers, writers, linguists and artists, pretested and their suitability affirmed before actual application.

— There are exercises at the end of every lesson and three tests in each primer.

— The entire exercise is based on the principle of self-evaluation and confidence (rather than competition) oriented evaluation. The tests are intended to be simple, non-threatening and participative.

— Every learner is free to attain the desired level according to his/her leisure and convenience. It is, however, expected that a learner should be able to complete all the three primers within the overall duration of 200 hours spread over 68 months.

Total Literacy Campaign

After the launch of NLM in 1988, between 1988 and 1990, the Mission tried to consolidate the earlier centre-based programme to make its implementation more effective. There was no change in the strategy and the centre-based programmes continued. The changes which were brought about in the reorganisation, mainly consisted of streamlining the various activities and correcting managerial deficiencies. Detailed guidelines for project formulation and implementation were laid down and administrative and supervisory control was vested with the state governments.

However, in spite of extensive revision of guidelines, the deficiencies earlier noticed, could not be remedied in the implementation process. One notable exception to the centre-based approach and an experiment with the campaign mode was first seen in Kottayam city in Kerala. Here the district collector, by mobilising 200 volunteers from the local university and forging links with 2000 non-literates in the 6-60 age group, succeeded in making them fully literate within three months.

But, the real breakthrough came with an experiment in mass literacy campaign initiated in 1989 and successfully completed in 1990 in Ernakulam district in Kerala. The campaign for total literacy here saw fusion between the district administration headed by its collector, volunteer groups, social activists and others, and was spearheaded by the Kerala Shastra Sahitya Parishad (KSSP). Ernakulam achieved this objective on 4th February 1990 and along with it, the unique distinction of being the first district in the country to become 'fully' literate.

The principal shift in strategy adopted in the Ernakulam experiment was a change to a well coordinated, comprehensive and identifiable initiative. It also marked a change by altering the social context in order to generate demand for the programme and further to sustain it. It established the feasibility of a mass- based, community-based, campaign approach with the objective of generating environment building and demand for literacy followed by literacy instruction. The subsequent adoption of the campaign has taken firm root and has given rise to the Total Literacy Campaign (TLC) approach. Drawing inspiration from the success achieved in Ernakulam, entire Kerala, Goa, UT of Pondicherry and several districts in Karnataka, Andhra Pradesh and West Bengal have taken up the challenge for achieving total literacy in a given time frame. These TLCs had a snowballing effect and campaigns were launched in quick succession all over the country.

The TLC model is now accepted as a dominant strategy of eradication of adult illiteracy by almost all States/UTs. This strategy has been reviewed and endorsed by the National Development Council and also by the conference of chief ministers of states by the Prime Minister on February 15, 1994. TLCs have certain features which make them unique and distinguish them from other government programmes:

(i) These campaigns are area-specific, time-bound, volunteer-based, cost-effective and outcome oriented. The thrust in TLCs is on attainment of predetermined norms of literacy and numeracy. The learner is the focal point in the entire process and measurement of learning outcome is continuous, informal, participative and non-threatening.

(ii) The campaigns are implemented through district level literacy committees which are registered under the Societies Registration Act as independent and autonomous bodies to provide a unified umbrella under which a number of individuals and organisations work together. The leadership to this body is provided by the district collector/chief secretary and zila parishad (district council). All sections of society are given due representation in the planning and implementation of the programme. On the basis of the Ernakulam experience, an organisational structure for a district TLC has been evolved. The structure rests on 3 pillars of (1) participatory people's committees; (2) full-time functionaries and area coordinators; and (3) a support system provided by government officials. In itself, this may not seem significant, but it exemplifies an interactive and a communicative process of management and implementation.

(iii) The campaign approach to total literacy is characterised by large scale mobilisation through a multifaceted communication strategy. The success of the campaign rests substantially on the effectiveness with which all sections of society are mobilised.

(iv) No targets are fixed from the top. The targets emanate from the grassroot level on the basis of a detailed door-to-door survey conducted by the volunteers. This survey is not only a headcounting exercise, but also a tool of planning, mobilisation and environment building.

(v) The campaign is delivered through volunteers without any expectation of reward or incentive.

(vi) The management information system in a campaign is based on the twin principles of participation and correction. It has, to be accountable, credible and instead of being enrolment oriented, it has to be outcome oriented.

(vii) To enable every learner to achieve measurable levels of literacy, the new pedagogy known as 'Improved Pace and Content of Learning (IPCL)" has been translated in the shape of a set of multigraded and integrated teaching-learning materials and training. The learner is placed at the focal point in the entire process which, through compact duration and continuous ongoing evaluation, helps to heighten the learner's motivation and improve the pace of learning.

(viii) Training of all functionaries involved in the campaign is crucial to the success of the campaign. Training has to be primer-specific, participative, communicative and a tool of continuous correction, upgradation and human resource development.

(ix) Though the TLC is meant to impart functional literacy, it also disseminates a 'basket' of other socially relevant messages such as enrolment and retention of children in schools, immunisation, propagation of small family norms, promotion of maternity and child care; women's equality and empowerment, peace and communal harmony etc.

At present, the system of monitoring and supervision comprises the following:

— District collectors/chairmen of the ZSSs furnish monthly progress reports in the prescribed proforma on the status of TLC/PLC in the districts to the state directorate of adult education and central directorate of adult education.

— Consolidated reports from the state directorate of adult education.

— Feedback received from the state chief secretaries/education secretaries on the basis of periodical review meetings with the district collectors.

— Visit reports of NLMA members, consultants and departmental officers.

— Internal and external evaluation reports.

EVALUATION OF LEARNING OUTCOMES

The evaluation of learning outcomes of those enrolled has been built in the body of multigraded primers. The primers are in three parts and at the end of every lesson, drills and exercises have been provided which are required to be attended intensively by every learner under the overall guidance of the volunteers. This self-evaluation enables the learner to perceive the pace and progress of learning himself and serves to heighten the motivation and consequently quicken the pace of learning.

In the light of experience gained in monitoring of literacy campaigns and a review of the evaluation practices, NLM has recently introduced a system of concurrent evaluation for an ongoing literacy project. This is a kind of quick mid-term appraisal of a project to assess the strength and weaknesses of an ongoing programme and suggest correctives. The guide lines by the NLM for concurrent evaluation require that these not be conducted by the implementing agency but by an outside agency, mostly institutions of social science research, whose panel is maintained by the State Directorate of Adult Education. On being approached, the State Director of Adult Education nominates the agency for conducting concurrent evaluation of a literacy project.

Besides concurrent evaluation, each TLC project is now subject to a final evaluation as soon as the literacy campaign is concluded or is about to conclude. The National Literacy Mission has identified a panel of reputed Social Science Research Institutions and these are empanelled as independent external evaluation agencies. The Zilla Saksharta Samitis (ZSSs) are expected to inform the NLM when they are ready for the external evaluation. The NLM in turn will nominate an appropriate external evaluation agency out of the empanelled agencies. The empanelled agencies are periodically briefed and oriented by the Directorate of Adult Education, Government of India, in regard to evaluation methodologies and techniques for realistic assessment of achievements. The new approach to evaluation adopted by the NLM emphasises upon ensuring complete transparency of the programme and thus enhances the credibility of the results reported by a district.

6

Planning and Policies for EFA

Colonial education was highly elitist and was therefore irrelevant to the needs of the masses. Educational efforts were more often directed towards developing an educated aristocracy that would provide a strong support base for sustaining the British rule in India. Ironically, it was because some, amongst these same 'enlightened' Indians, noticed that the British had introduced free and compulsory education in their country, that the demand for the same arose in India. This demand was later articulated by the nationalists who realised the political importance of educating the masses in order to overthrow the colonial regime. Gopal Krishan Gokhale, noted freedom fighter, was one of the first to emphasise the need for mass education. However, the Bill he introduced on compulsory education where he demanded that the local bodies should take the initiative in the matter, met with resistance so that only half-hearted efforts were made by the British to introduce compulsory education in India.

It was for Mahatma Gandhi to pick up the threads, some twenty years later. He realised that education at the village level was very essential if the people were to overthrow the yoke of the British rule. However, the strength in Gandhi's ideas lay in the fact that apart from making people politically aware, education had a significant role in making them sensitive to the social evils like the caste system, Sati, untouchability, and superstitious beliefs. Gandhi's self-financing scheme of Basic Education aimed at making education relevant for the village community, hence an antithesis to the elitist colonial education.

Basic education system as evolved by Mahatma Gandhi, was one of the important goals of the freedom struggle. In the Constitution of India, adopted in 1950, elementary education received explicit attention. The Directive Principle contained in Article 45 of the Constitution directed the State to "endeavour to provide, within a period of ten years from the commencement of this Constitution, for free and compulsory education for all children until they complete the age of fourteen years." Alongside, equality of opportunity was also given primacy through various other articles (e.g. Article 29(2) dealt with the right to admission into any educational institution maintained by the state, Article 350-A laid down the right to receive instruction in the mother tongue, Article 46 referred to taking care of the economic and educational interests of the under-privileged sections of the population, etc.) Subsequently, fourteen states and four UTs (Union Territories) enacted the legislation for compulsory primary education. But since education was a state subject, the centre could not prevail upon the states to enforce compulsion. The states also found that in practice this legislation was difficult to implement due to various constraints.

With regard to the education of adults, on the other hand, there was no such explicit Constitutional commitment. Rather, there seemed to be an implicit understanding that over the years the expansion of primary education would automatically take care of the problem of mass illiteracy.

How was the political commitment reflected. in the Constitutional Directive to provide free and compulsory education to children in the 6-14 age group, translated into action? In order to understand this, it would be necessary to analyse policy documents to see how this mandate was articulated in various education policies as well as in the plan documents, and to see what were the financial resources that were allocated.

In the Constitution of India, adopted in 1950, elementary education received explicit attention. The Directive Principle contained in Article 45 of the Constitution directed the State to "endeavour to provide, within a period of ten years from the commencement of this Constitution, for free and compulsory education for all children until they complete the age of fourteen years."

Immediately after independence, Indian planning had to contend with three competing claims: the Constitutional obligation regarding eight years of compulsory education, the manpower needs of a growing economy and the growing demand for expansion of educational institutions. In 1947, when the country achieved independence, there was no accepted plan of a national system of education. Three definite steps were therefore expected of the government that came to power viz. (a) to prepare a blueprint of a national system of education (b) allocate sufficient financial resources (c) transform the entire educational system so that all educational institutions became national schools. All this, however, did not take place and there was merely a linear expansion of the existing educational system through allocation of financial resources to this system. It was in the late fifties and early sixties, that a strong demand was made that the Government of India set up an Education Commission, that looked at education holistically and which also included primary and adult education. It was in response to-this demand that the Central government appointed the Education Commission (1964-66) and entrusted it with the task of looking at the entire system of education so that a national system of education would emerge.

The report of the Education Commission recommended a radical transformation in the prevailing education system and suggested that it should be related to life, to the needs and aspirations of the people, and that there should be a qualitative improvement in its standards and a quantitative expansion of educational opportunities on the basis of manpower needs and equalisation of educational opportunities. While reiterating Article 45 of the Constitutional commitment, but in view of the tremendous human and financial resources that this mandate entailed, it recommended that elementary education be phased by providing 5 years of effective education to all children by 1975-76 and 7 years of such education by 1985-86.

The first National Policy on Education was formulated only in July 1968. In many ways, the policy diluted the recommendations of the Education Commission. On the one hand, Article 45 was emphasised and most of the recommendation$ of the Commission were incorporated, such as free and compulsory education, equalisation of educational opportunities including education for girls, spread of literacy and adult education through literacy campaigns etc. But at the same time, the policy was somewhat ambivalent about the overall importance of mass education. Also, one of the major problems of the policy was that it did not articulate how the policy directives could be translated into action.

The plan allocations for education in general have never been adequate. But even within the education budget, the tension between the Constitutional commitment to provide free and compulsory education to all children in the 6-14 age group and the development imperative of training skilled manpower through provision of higher and technical education, has persisted through the years. Thus, while every commission and committee on education during the post-independence period reiterated the importance of fulfilling the Constitutional obligation, and every Five Year Plan attempted to reach this goal, in reality the share of higher and technical education continuously increased from the First Five Year plan to 1968-69. To some extent, the perception that elementary education was a 'public good' and a welfare activity to be provided by the government and that higher and technical education war, a crucial factor for economic development, tilted the balance in favour of the latter. Thus, the share of higher education continued to remain high even during the Fourth, Fifth and Sixth Five Year Plans.

In the case of adult education, on the other hand, there was an official recognition of the link between primary and adult education. The First Five Year Plan, for instance, had observed that 'the programme of primary education is considerably handicapped without a corresponding programme of the education of adults'. But the emphasis was laid on the rapid expansion of the formal school system, and adult education was relegated to a relatively unimportant position in the general scheme of education. As a result, the financial allocations were meagre in the First, Second and Third Five Year Plans. Throughout the 1960s, various government committees drew attention to the urgent need to tackle the problem of adult illiteracy. By far the most comprehensive of these was the Report of the Education Commission (1964-66). The Commission urged that it was the failure of the formal system of education that had necessitated a two-pronged strategy of educating the children as well as the adults. Also, it was realised that the demand for the education of children could be generated only if the adults were made literate.

Even with regard to education of girls and women, while there was an awareness of persistent illiteracy and wide male-female gaps, there was a general feeling that increasing and expanding infrastructure and supply would automatically enhance access.

This was true up to a point- female enrolment increased phenomenally in the first three decades. But one of the serious omissions was the inability to address persistent gender, caste and community based disparities in access. As a result, women belonging to some socioeconomic groups, especially in backward regions of the country, were left out of the formal stream of education. Declining resource allocation for adult education notwithstanding, the government appointed numerous commissions and committees since 1950 to consider and study the problem of women's education and innumerable reports were tabled in Parliament and discussed in the Planning Commission. These documents recognised that the major stumbling block for the participation of women was their poverty and that women from poor communities, especially in rural areas, needed special attention. Various strategies, starting from flexible school timings to decentralised planning and administration were recommended time and again in these reports.

The rapid and unplanned expansion of higher education resulted in deterioration of standards and creation of problems of educated unemployed youth. In elementary education, on the other hand, problems of wastage and stagnation continued as no major structural changes were made in the existing educational system. It was at this juncture that the National Policy on

Education, along with its Programme of Action, was enunciated. Based on an in-depth review of educational performance in the country and formulated through an intensive process of nation-wide consultation, the NPE 1986, redefined educational priorities and made a new attempt to cope with three strands that have influenced educational policy in India viz. those relating to issues of Quantity, quality and equity.

The National Policy on Education gave the highest priority to universalisation of elementary education and adult education. While this was reflected in the higher allocation of resources, other measures were also included to improve the overall quality of the educational system such as giving as much importance to retention and levels of achievement as enrolment, and focusing on the more difficult aspects of access-such as ensuring access to girls and the disadvantaged groups. There was also the realisation of the need for people's involvement through the setting up of the village education committee. The Policy reiterated the need for decentralisation in education, keeping the district as the basic unit for planning and management. It was also during this period that World Bank and other international donor agencies started emphasising the need to invest in education of girls as the only way to address issues of population growth, maternal and child health, and mortality and morbidity-related issues.

The National Policy on Education gave the highest priority to universalisation of elementary education and adult education. There was also the realisation of the need for people's involvement through the setting up of the village education committees. The Policy reiterated the need for decentralisation in education, keeping the district as the basic unit for planning and management.

The educational priorities enunciated by NPE, 1986, have continued through the 90s. This is reflected in the higher financial allocations that have been made to elementary and adult education in recent years. The graphs below show how the priorities in financial allocations have changed over the years.

Political commitment to EFA found an expression in the manifestos of the political parties in the last general elections. Thus, the manifestos of most political parties expressed a strong commitment to promote the education of children as well as of adults.

Reaffirmation of the political commitment is also reflected in the Common Minimum Programme (CMP) of the present government which resolved to make right to free and compulsory education a fundamental right and to enforce it through suitable statutory measures.

The Committee of State Education Ministers which was set up to examine the implications of the aforesaid resolution recommended that the Constitution be amended to make the right to free and compulsory education from six to fourteen years of age a fundamental right and to make it a fundamental duty of the parents to provide opportunities for education to children of this age group. A Constitutional Amendment Bill has been tabled in the Parliament, in July 1997, to give effect to these recommendations. When passed, states and Union Territories would be required to enact laws for the enforcement of free and compulsory education within one year from the commencement of the Constitution (Eighty-third Amendment) Act, 1997.

Elementary Education System

The elementary education system in India has become one of the largest in the world with 150.74 million children enrolled in 1995-96 in the age-group of 6-14 years covering about 91 per cent of the children in this age group. Of these, 109.73 million children were enrolled in 5,90,421 primary schools and 41.01 million in 1,71,216 upper primary schools. There are 2.90 million teachers-1.74 million employed in primary schools and 1.16 million in upper primary schools. 95 per cent of rural population living in 8.26 lakh habitations have a school within a walking distance of 1 km. and 84 per cent have upper primary schooling facility within a walking distance of 3 kms.

While these could be regarded as impressive achievements, what is disquieting are the low retention as well as low achievement levels. According to the government statistics, the drop-out rate at the primary level is decreasing. Yet, it is still as high as 36.3 per cent for primary schools and 52.7 per cent for upper primary level for 1994-95. On the other hand, various studies have shown that the levels of learner achievement are rather low.

Also, national averages tend to mask wide regional disparities. While the proportion of never-enrolled children has declined in all states, the proportion is still quite high in the states of Bihar, Rajasthan, Uttar Pradesh and Madhya Pradesh. A significant gap between male and female literacy rates continues to remain despite intensive efforts to bridge it. In 1995-96, girls accounted for only 43.2 per cent of the total enrolment at the primary stage and 39 per cent at the upper primary stage. The drop out rate of girls is much higher than that of boys at the primary and upper primary stages. Similarly, there is a need to improve the overall enrolment and retention rates among the children of the socially and economically disadvantaged groups such as the Scheduled Castes and Scheduled Tribes. The proportion of out-of- school and working children is extremely high.

The elementary education system in India has become one of the largest in the world with 150.74 million children enrolled in 1995-96 in the age-group of 6-14 years covering about 91 percent of the children in this age group. In order to achieve Universalisation of Elementary Education (UEE) by the year 2000, the following strategies have been worked out in consultation with the States and the Union Territories:-

a) overcome the problem of school dropouts and lay emphasis on retention and achievement rather than on merely enrolment;

b) strengthen the alternatives of schooling, particularly the Non-Formal Education system for working children, girls and children from other disadvantaged and marginalised sections of the society;

c) shift focus from educationally backward States to educationally backward districts;

d) population specific plans;

e) provide universal access to schooling facilities, particularly to girls disadvantaged groups and out-of-school children;

f) improve school effectiveness, teacher competence, training and motivation;

g) introduce Minimum Levels of Learning (MLL) for enhancement of learners' achievement;

h) adopt micro planning strategies through the use of participatory processes; and

i) bring about a convergence of different schemes of elementary education and related services such as early childhood care and education and school health and nutrition programmes.

System of Adult Education

In the post-independence period, the literacy rate has shown a substantial increase from about 16.7 per cent in

1951 to 52.2 per cent in 1991 for the 7+ population. As with elementary education, here too, there are sharp gender and regional disparities. There are wide regional variations from near-universal literacy in Kerala to 38.4 per cent in Bihar. There are also intrastate variations. The female literacy rate is 39.2 per cent as against 64.1 per cent for males. Furthermore, the literacy rates among the socially and economically disadvantaged groups (Scheduled Castes and Scheduled Tribes) are distinctly lower than that of the population as a whole. The gender disparity is also conspicuous among these groups.

The Total Literacy Campaigns were launched in 1990 with the goal of making literate 100 million non-literates by 1999. After the successful experience of Ernakulum, the TLCs have now covered 429 districts to reach out to 127 million people. Out of 88.48 million learners who were enrolled, 63.64 million have been made literate. Of these, 61 per cent were female and 39 per cent were male learners.

The Total Literacy Campaigns were launched in 1990 with the goal of making literate 100 million non-literates by 1999. After the successful experience of Ernakulum, the TLCs have now covered 429 districts to reach out to 127 million people. Out of 88.48 million learners who were enrolled, 63.64 million have been made literate. Of these, 61 percent were female and 39 percent were male learners.

As a follow-up to the TLCs, post literacy campaigns have been taken up in 193 districts. They are aimed at taking the neo-lilterates from a dependent to self-guided learning stage as well as promoting the development of income-generating skills. Continuing Education Programme has been initiated in 36 districts to provide access to all adults for life-long learning. These centres provide facilities such as a reading room and a library, skills improvement programme, a window for information dissemination, a centre for recreation and a place for organising cultural activities.

The substantial achievements since independence notwithstanding, India has the largest number of illiterates and out-of-school children in the world-37 per cent of the world's illiterates (in 1991) and 21.8 per cent of out-of-school children. In terms of actual numbers, 110.90 million adults, in the 15-35 age group were illiterate in 1991, of whom 61 per cent were women. In 1995-96, at least 63 million children in the 6-14 age group were out of school, of whom about 60 per cent were girls. Given the increasing demographic pressures, these numbers are likely to increase further. Also, the high infant mortality and maternal mortality rates, adverse sex ratio, and conservatism of social attitudes towards education of girls, have further exacerbated the problem of universalisation of education.

Due to the enormity of the problem, there has been a growing realisation of the need to make education a societal responsibility whereby all sections take the responsibility for dealing with this educational challenge. Alongside, there has been a realisation that the existing organisational structures and institutions that are rigid and hierarchical, have not been effective and that alternate structures need to be created that are more facilitative and enabling so that the participation of various sections can become possible.

The section below tries to capture various trends that have surfaced in recent years, both within the country as well as internationally, that have influenced educational thinking in this decade. Prominent among this development is the focus on political and social mobilisation for EFA.

Political and Social Mobilisation For EFA

In 1959, Gram Shikshan Mohim (Village Literacy Movement) was initiated in Maharashtra, first on an experimental basis in Satara district, and extended to all the districts of the state. With the Chief Minister taking a personal interest, the involvement of the entire government machinery and coordination between various departments at various levels-district, block and village-was ensured. But the crucial element in the programme was the manner in which the entire village community was successfully encouraged to participate in the campaign. Mass meetings were held in village after village, participation of the educated people of the village was elicited, and various strategies were used for the successful implementation of the campaign. In many ways, the Gram Shikshan Mohim anticipated some of the basic elements of the Total Literacy Campaign (TLC) which was first taken up in Ernakulum district of Kerala in 1989. The success of the literacy campaign in Ernakulum led to a considerable revision in the strategy of the National Literacy Mission. Also, some of the earlier adult education programmes such as the Farmers' Functional Literacy Programme (in late 60s) and the National Adult Education Programme (in late 70s) had shown that community support was critical for the success of any adult education programme. Thus, it was realised that the mass campaign had to be based on mass mobilisation and support of the government (both central and state), district administration, non-government and voluntary organisations, people from all sections of society and from all walks of life and that a spirit of voluntarism had to be the hallmark of the campaign.

Interestingly, the experience of the Total Literacy Campaign, based on the experience of the Kerala Sashtra Sahitya Parishad, an NGO working on popularisation of science among the villagers, coincided with the experience of countries that had undertaken literacy campaigns to deal with the problem of mass illiteracy. A study commissioned by UNESCO in the early 1980s-the findings of which were shared at an international meeting in Udaipur in 1982, highlighted some of the basic ingredients that were responsible for the success of the literacy campaigns. One of the major findings related to the importance of political will for the success of the literacy campaigns. The study showed that without its clear expression by a society's leaders, a successful campaign was most unlikely. While emphasising the ideological underpinnings of political will, the study also highlighted how all societies are capable of ideological commitment and can draw upon the cultural, moral, and spiritual resources of the people by challenging them to action and mobilising them around nationally defined issues.

Alongside, mobilisation of the masses and of the state also needed to take place to ensure the success of the mass literacy campaign. This was seen as a popular expression of the leadership's political will. No mass literacy campaign had succeeded without mass mobilisation, including that of personnel and resources within the government and in the political system.

The experience of the Total Literacy Campaigns (TLCs) in the late 80s- early 90s validated the importance of political and social mobilisation for initiating a process of social churning whereby a favourable environment for literacy could get created and literacy could find a place on the national agenda.

In 1990, UNESCO took the initiative, together with the World Bank, UNICEF, and UNDP, to organise at Jomtien, Thailand, the World Conference on Education for All. This marked the starting point for an unprecedented mobilisation of the international community on behalf of education. This cooperation has continued at the major conferences organised by the United Nations in recent years.

The Jomtien conference injected an urgent challenge into the educational landscape, and spelt out the movement's principles and strategies. Born out of the Jomtien conference, the leaders of the nine most populous countries of the world came together in the need to make education a societal responsibility, came out of a growing realisation that the sheer scale of achieving education for all entailed an entirely different way of conceiving and managing learning, away from a top-heavy, centralised model toward a more decentralised, democratic one.

Delhi in December 1993 and reaffirmed their commitment to pursue the goals set in Jomtien and at the World Summit for Children. One of the philosophical underpinnings of the EFA movement that received endorsement from these leaders was that of the need to forge alliances between different sectors of society, including students, parents, teachers and the community, along with the media, industry and different levels of government.

The need to make education a societal responsibility, came out of a growing realisation that the sheer scale of achieving education for all entailed an entirely different way of conceiving and managing learning, away from a top-heavy, centralised model toward a more decentralised, democratic one. There was also a realisation that beyond high-level political commitment, the goals for EFA would not be achieved without a strong degree of social mobilisation, meaning people's participation through organised and systematic actions. But for people to participate, structures of governance had to become more flexible and responsive to local needs. Also, the trend towards democratisation had to be accompanied by a gradual decentralisation of power from the central government to the states, districts and villages.

Independent India's attempt to bring about democratic decentralisation dates back to the days of the community development programme that of the community development programme that was launched in 1952. Thereafter in the early 1960s, most of the states passed the Panchayati Raj Acts. However, after the initial enthusiasm, interest of the states in democratic decentralisation waned. It was only in 1992 that the 73rd and 74th amendment of the Indian Constitution opened a new chapter in the process of democratic decentralisation by making it mandatory for all states to establish regular democratically elected bodies for local self-government. The National Policy on Education (1986) and the Programme of Action which were revised in 1992, while noting the constitutional amendments, suggested, among other things, the constitution of a village education committee:

> "... which would be responsible for administration of delegated powers in the field of education at the village level."

Its major responsibility being the:

> "... operationalisation of micro-level planning and school mapping in the village through systematic house-to-house survey and periodic discussions with the parents."

For these and other functions it would be necessary to vest village education committees with appropriate statutory and necessary financial and administrative authority. The Programme of Action suggested that the state government would consider entrusting these committees with the following functions :

> "...generating and sustaining awareness among the village community, ensuring participation of all segments of population; and developing teacher/ instructor and community partnership to oversee and manage the effective and regular functioning of the schools and centres."

EFA INITIATIVES

The World Conference on Education for All, held in Jomtien in 1990, is a landmark in that it unfolded the possibility of donor assistance for basic education. Donors recognised that investing in human resources paid rich economic dividends. Education of the girl child was particularly seen as a positive contributing factor in controlling population growth. Policy makers and planners who had earlier been arguing for greater allocations for elementary education realised that they could mobilise additional resources through foreign aid. As a result, a wide range of education programmes and projects were introduced with bilateral assistance. By 1992, the World Bank emerged as a major player in the education scenario. Prior to 1990, a few pilot projects had been designed to address certain facets of basic education. Among these were:-

— Andhra Pradesh Primary Education Project for improving classroom transaction by training teachers to adopt more child-centre and activity oriented approaches. The project also undertook construction of 3,255 classrooms and 1,070 teacher centres (with British ODA assistance).

— Mahila Samakhya—an education programme for women's empowerment (with the assistance from the Government of Netherlands)

— Shiksha Karmi Project which aimed at providing learning opportunities by recruiting local volunteers in remote villages where teacher absenteeism was high (with SIDA assistance)

The UNICEF-assisted Bihar Education Project (BEP) set the pace for comprehensive projects aimed at restructuring of primary education as a whole in selected districts. BEP was followed by Lok Jumbish in Rajasthan also with SIDA assistance. The concept of comprehensive district-based projects came of age with the launching of the District Primary Education Project (DPEP)- the primary education project that has received financial support from.IDA. Total Literacy Campaigns (TLCs) that have been launched by the National Literacy Mission, however, have not received any foreign funding.

An attempt is made below to describe some of these initiatives that have focussed on political and social mobilisation for achieving the goal of education for all.

National Literacy Mission

The establishment of the National Literacy Mission in 1988 gave to literacy and adult education, primacy of place on the national agenda. Then in 1990, came the unique experiment in Ernakulum district of Kerala where a campaign approach was adopted This was characterised by large scale mobilisation of people from all walks of life through a multifaceted communication strategy that highlighted the vital link between literacy and living. The essence of the campaign was to generate a positive demand for learning as a tool for social change. The campaign for total literacy that was spearheaded by Kerala Shastra Sahitya Parishad- an NGO working for popularising science among villagers-demonstrated how an alliance and a partnership could be established between the bureaucracy at the district level on the one hand, and the social activists and volunteer groups on the other. The successful experience of Ernakulum gave birth to the concept of Total Literacy Campaign (TLC) in the 90s. Total Literacy Campaign is a planned, coordinated and comprehensive district level drive, with identified time-bound objectives. It has a target of making 100 million people in the 15-35 age group literate by 1999.

The National Literacy Mission has a three-tiered structure. At the national and state level are the National and State Literacy Mission Authority that support and provide direction to the programme. At the district level, an autonomous organisation called the Zilla Saksharta Samiti, is registered to provide a forum for individuals and organisations to work together. This samiti often constitutes a mix of government officials, elected political leaders, NGOs, representatives of mass organisations, including women's organisations. In most districts, the Collector becomes the chairperson of the Zilla Saksharta Samiti (ZSS) as he/she is then able to galvanise the support of different development departments in the implementation of the TLC. The Bharat Gyan Vigyan Samiti (BGVS) a national NGO with state level groups, has been providing on-going support to TLCs.

The initiation of the TLC begins with a process of consultation and consensus-building between government officials, political leaders, teachers and students, activist groups, cultural troupes. After the setting up of the Zilla Saksharta Samiti, a detailed survey is conducted in the district to enumerate and identify the non-literate people. The process of conducting the survey also provides opportunities for person to person contact and interaction, as well as for identifying-the literacy volunteers and master trainers. The innovative aspect of the TLC model is the emphasis that is put on the creation of a favourable environment for literacy. This environment building phase consists of the use of traditional folk media forms and of 'kalajathas' that consist of cultural troupes that perform street corner plays. Conventional media like the electronic media, press, posters, banners, hoardings and other nontraditional forms such as padayatras, prabhat pheris, are all used with great effect. The basic objective of the environment building phase is to mobilise public opinion, sensitise the educated sections of the community so that they come forward as literacy volunteers and mobilise and motivate the non- literate adults to participate as learners in the literacy campaign.

Political support from all political parties is ensured by involving the political leaders in organisational structures that are set up and in the events that are specially organised to sustain the momentum that is generated for the literacy campaign. Social mobilisation is attempted by garnering support for the campaign from different sections of the society by setting up support structures that provide technical resource support to the campaign.

After the success of the Ernakulum experiment in Kerala, the TLC model has now been used to cover 429 out of India's 520 districts. Adult literacy programmes were earlier considered a welfare activity to be performed by the adult education department. This mindset has undergone a change for there is a growing realisation that the problem of illiteracy is a societal responsibility and that partnerships have to be forged between the bureaucracy, different sections of the society and the community. Experience has generally shown that women have participated in TLCs in large numbers.

With the emphasis on mobilisation, women have received a social sanction to participate in the literacy campaign without the hindrance of their husbands and their parents-in-law. The experience of the anti-arrack agitation that was spearheaded by the village women of the Nellore district of Andhra Pradesh has shown how the literacy campaign provided the impetus to women to organise against a social evil that plagued their lives and affected the well-being of their families.

In Puddukotai district of Tamil Nadu, as the village women started to participate in the literacy campaign, they learnt how to ride a bicycle and thereby felt empowered as they became physically mobile. In a large number of districts, the TLCs reduced the distance between the Collector and other district level officials, and the poor and the disadvantaged groups. For vast sections of poor people, TLCs provided an opportunity to make their voices heard before the district administration. Another positive impact has been the impetus they have provided to primary education. It has been reported that enrolment and retention levels have increased after a TLC.

Political support from all political parties in ensured by involving the political leaders in organisational structures and events. Social mobilisation is attempted by garnering support for the campaign from different sections of the society.

NLM has visualised the post literacy programme as an extension of the TLC in the continuum of lifelong learning. Each TLC is followed by a two-year post literacy programme, to be implemented in a mission mode. After the completion of this phase, an institutionalised mechanism for continuing education through continuing education centres is provided to enable the neo-literate adults to retain, improve and apply their basic knowledge and skills in fulfilling their needs and aspirations.

The TLCs have brought about a tremendous social awakening in some districts. But sustaining the momentum of the campaign is proving to be difficult. This calls for creative responses for ensuring that the community is involved in different ways so that the community gradually begins to take charge of the programme. If this does not happen, then there is the danger of routinisation and ritualising of the processes that would rob community participation of its essential vitality and spontaneity. In the Hindi belt (comprising the states of Rajasthan, Madhya Pradesh, Bihar and Uttar Pradesh), on the other

Continuing Education

The literacy campaign was launched in Birbhum is 1990 and was implemented with full involvement of the people and the district administration working together in a spirit of cooperation. The literacy campaign has brought the officials closer to the people and to their problems. Community members are no longer hesitant to contribute to the development plans of their region. They have welcomed the plans for opening continuing education centres in every village. These multi-service centres would provide library facilities, literacy instruction, quality of life improvement programmes, skill development schemes and would also function as information windows disseminating useful, life related information.

Birbhum has high percentage of forest cover. For the women of the district, this provides economic opportunity. They collect leaves from the forest, stitching them together to make disposable plates. The demand for these plates is considerable and gives to the women a small but continuous source of income. The literacy programme has taught them to put part of their earnings in banks. Thus times of need they now have access to micro-credit.

Due to an effective literacy campaign, enrolment in primary schools showed a marked improvement. People are more interested in education now . The impact has also been felt in health programmes, immunisation and the adoption of family planning measures. In recent times, the community stood together and combated what was threatening to become an epidemic of gastroenteritis.

The campaign also spread awareness and promoted more access to information about development schemes. New opportunities to augment income through pisiculture have come up. The community, through voluntary labour, has dug fishery tanks in this region which provides people of this largely fish eating area with a nutritious diet as well as additional income.

On the other hand, the TLC model has shown how in a deeply entrenched feudal and patriarchal society, factors such as caste, class and gender divide, can militate against meaningful community participation. As a result, it is difficult to elicit community support and participation and there has been over reliance on the initiative and drive shown by the bureaucracy.

These experiences have highlighted the need for decentralisation and delegation of power and authority. The new strategies envisage devolution of power for approval/implementation of literacy programmes to State Literacy Mission Authorities, establishing strong linkages between literacy campaigns and Panchayati Raj institutions, involvement of the Panchayati Raj functionaries in the literacy movement and establishment of strong linkages between the literacy programme and other development programmes.

Shiksha Karmi and Lok Jumbish

The Lok Jumbish and Shiksha Karmi Projects are integral and strategic components of renewed and intensified efforts of the Government of Rajasthan for achieving the goal of basic education for all.

To overcome the problem of teacher absenteeism, the concept of 'barefoot teachers' was introduced by the Shiksha Karmi Project (SKP) which is being implemented in Rajasthan since 1987 with financial assistance from Swedish International Development Cooperation Agency

(SIDA). The idea was to substitute the absent primary school teacher by a female and male 'local educational worker' who would have a certain level of education, but no prior teaching experience. The project aims at universalisation and qualitative improvement of primary education in remote and socio-economically backward villages in Rajasthan, with primary attention being given to girls. The project is being implemented by the Government of Rajasthan through Rajasthan Shiksha Karmi Board, with assistance of voluntary agencies. SKP works on the following assumptions:-

— that a 'barefoot teacher' belonging to a local community can work effectively to reach every child in the locality;

— that if a person is willing to work as a social worker, the lack of formal educational qualifications can be made up by intensive in-service education and training; and

— that education must have community support and local ownership in order to meet the needs of the deprived sections of the rural areas.

An important role has been given to voluntary organisations and the community in providing continuous support and encouragement to the Shiksha Karmis. SKP has constituted Village Education Committees (VECs) to promote community involvement in primary education and encourage village level planning. The role of the VEC is to mobilise resources for maintenance, repair and construction of school infrastructure.

In many villages, SKs have been able to mobilise local support for the school buildings. In village Raymalvada of Osian panchayat samiti, a very good piece of land has been donated for SK school by a community member. In village Bharla of Arain panchayat samiti also, a villager has donated a substantial piece of land for the SK school. In Lunkaransar panchyat samiti, some people have made financial contributions as well as given major support for the construction of the school building the Day Schools and Prehar Pathshalas (schools of convenient timing). The VEC helps in determining the school calendar and school timings in consultation with the local community and the Shiksha Karmis. They also identify local talent i.e. story tellers, musicians and artists who can be associated with enrichment of teaching process in the Day Schools and Prehar Pathshalas. The VEC assists Shiksha Karmis in running the village/school library. The SKP places funds at the disposal of the VEC to be utilised for minor repairs of the school buildings. The funds are released by Shiksha Karmi Board in proportion to the money raised by VECs.

Apart from the VEC, NGOs also assist the Shiksha Karmi Board in implementation of the project. They are the local resource base for SKP and have the following functions:

(i) assist in identification and selection of villages and Shiksha Karmis;

(ii) facilitate formation of VECs

(iii) assist in training and evaluation

(iv) assist Resource Units in the modification of curriculum for local relevance

(v) provide training in local communication skills to Shiksha Karmis

(vi) establish and run Resource Units on the basis of their capabilities, past experience, presence of physical infrastructure and availability of human resources

(vii) run Mahila Prashikshan Kendras (residential schools for women)

(viii) run Aangan Pathshalas (courtyard schools) for girls in their neighbourhood

(ix) review and participate in evaluation activities on a continuing basis.

It is the community support and the participation of the NGOs that has helped in improving the physical conditions and the environment of the primary schools, as well as in promoting the education of the girls. Different strategies have been used to improve the status of girls' education, as enrolment, attendance and retention of girls is the major challenge in the project. Some of the strategies include :

— increasing the number of female SKs and to have one female SK (Mahila Shiksha Karmi) in each school; and

— starting special residential schools for women, Mahila Prashikshan Kendras (MPKs) as there are not enough women with sufficient education. In these schools women go through intensive training for two years in order to reach the level of five years of education;

— starting special night schools, or rather schools of convenient timings, Prehar Pathshalas (PPs);

— introducing female escorts, Mahila Sahyogis (MSs) to accompany girls in remote places between home and school, and to take care of the girls' siblings during school hours; and

— starting courtyard schools adapted to girls, Aangan Pathshalas (APs) in remote villages. The school is run by a female SK.

SKP is now operational in 2,000 villages in 127 blocks of 29 districts of Rajasthan. There has been a 300 per cent increase in enrolment of children in the 6-14 age group in Shiksha Karmi schools and Prehar Pathshalas (PPs) from

30,000 at the time of taking over under SKP to 1,58,568 at present. One of the outstanding achievements of SKP is 100 per cent enrolment of children in the 6-14 age group in 469 villages.

Lately, SKP is in the process of reducing its direct involvement. The strategy is to achieve maximum decentralisation by providing a regional support structure for better management. For this purpose, resource units are now functioning as core management groups comprising of SKs, master trainers and mahila sahayogis. This resource unit enjoys the autonomy to implement the programme within the framework of the established norms.

Lok Jumbish translates as a movement of the people. It has a holistic understanding about the problem of universalising primary education and is implemented by establishing an interface between the local community, the teaching profession, the educational administration and the learners.

This project was initiated in 1992 and is now operational in 75 blocks of 27 districts of Rajasthan. It is funded by Swedish International Development Cooperation, Agency ($IDA), Government of India and the state government in the ratio of 3:2:1. An independent autonomous body, the Lok Jumbish Parishad has been set up for the management of this programme. The general council and the executive committee have representatives from the Ministry of Human Resource Development, Government of Rajasthan, Teachers' Associations and NGOs. Block level management committees have been set up for decentralised decision- making and implementation. Review and planning meetings are held once in every two months and selected clusters in blocks have been entrusted to NGOs . Lok Jumbish works closely with the teachers and their associations. The teachers are given a 10 day training initially, followed by monthly workshops and a 3-week specialised training every year.

Lok Jumbish translates as a movement of the people. It has a holistic understanding about the problem of universalising primary education and is implemented by establishing an interface between the local community, the teaching profession, the educational administration and the learners. The goals of Lok Jumbish are the following:

— providing access to primary education to all children upto 14 years of age;

— ensuring that all enrolled children regularly attend school/sahaj shiksha (Non-Formal Education) centres and complete primary education;

— ensuring that the quality of education is improved and that all children achieve at least the minimum levels of learning;

— creating necessary structures and setting in motion processes that would empower women and make education an instrument of women's equality;

— pursuing the goal of equity in education;

— making necessary modifications in the content and process of education in order that they relate better to the environment, people's culture and to their living and working conditions; and

— effectively involve people in the planning and management of education.

In order to reach the above goals, the following guiding principles have been enunciated:

— emphasis on the process of learning and not just the output;

— building partnerships;

— decentralised functioning;

— participatory learning;
— integration with the mainstream education system;
— flexibility of management; and
— creation of multiple levels of leadership committed to quality and mission mode.

Community participation not only involves the villagers, teachers and the field staff and students but also NGOs. Apart from community involvement at the local level, at the macro level, it involves consultants in the fields of basic education, pedagogy, gender, community development, management, educational planning and architecture. This is indicative of the growing need.

The VEC has its roots in the core group (Prerak Dal) of concerned villagers that is formed as an "activating agency" to mobilise the community. The teacher forms the center of the core team. It also includes functionaries of development programmes at the village level. The core team expands into the VEC, taking into its wings elected ward members and the head of the Gram Panchayat (the Sarpanch). A part of the VEC is the mahila Samooh, a collective of village women.

The Mahila Samoohs focus on girls' enrolment and retention in school and also act a focal point for women's access to development projects. It comprises of respected women in the village representing all castes.

Mapping exercises, door-to-door surveys and regular, periodic discussions with all villagers, especially parents and adults illiterates, mark the beginning of the VEC's work.

Mapping exercises have raised the awareness of marginalised and disadvantaged communities. They have also highlighted the improvement in the quality of life of families whose children are school-goers. At one level, it has managed to being a long-overdue process of social integration. At another level, it has encouraged individual families to break with tradition and send children to school.

The insistence of surveying all homes has brought the underprivileged sections within the ambit of education. It also begins a process of breaking down age-old barriers, which, in many cases, socially ostracised some segments of the community.

Each VEC sets up a village education fund. for specialists in various aspects of education for making interventions at the grass-root level.

Community involvement is the key factor for the success of the project. The Village Education Committees (VECs)/Core Teams and Women's Groups, carefully formed and trained through environment building activities in the LJ programme, are actively involved in school-mapping and micro-planning. School Building committees (Bhawan Nirman Samitis) plan and organise repair, maintenance and design of school buildings. These committees consist of at least two women members, the school teacher, members of the VEC, the mason and the architect. The aim is to train local people to take the responsibility for the design, management and execution of the building development programme. This culture of participation would in the long run, help in taking up the maintenance of school infrastructure at the village level. Villagers have already started devising innovative ways of making a contribution in cash and in kind.

Mobilising the village community to take responsibility to ensure quality education for every child, is the core strategy of U. In the first phase, mobilisation efforts are focused on identification of cultural groups, making door-to-door contact and creating an atmosphere for discussing educational issues. Regular visits to the selected villages are made over a long period of time by the LJ staff. Through this interaction, the confidence of the villagers is gained and potential volunteers who will work towards improving education, are identified. These individuals, men and women, gradually assume the responsibility of becoming the Core Team.

Women's groups have been mobilised in the villages where environment building activities have taken place. The gathering of women to discuss social and economic problems has created an entry point for discussions on the need for girls' education. Articulate women are hand-picked to participate in a five-day training programme. After completion of the training, these women form a women's group, mahila samooh, which assumes the role of a catalyst in the village.

Members of women's groups and core teams receive training focused on analysing the problems of education at the village level within the context of overall development, e.g. lack of drinking water might be identified as a problem along with the lack of school building. The training and environment building activities prepare the community to carry out school mapping and micro-planning.

Core team members learn how to carry out school mapping and involve a large section of the village in this process. All children in the 5- 14 age group are identified, their educational status noted and the nature of work done by out-of-school children is recorded. Simple symbols are used to record all aspects so that non-literate villagers can participate in the exercise. The information gathered through school mapping is shared at the village meetings. At the end of the process, a Village Education Plan is prepared. The plans are forwarded to the Block Management Committee for approval.

In the formation of the core teams, adequate representation of women is insisted upon; similarly, it is generally ensured that persons from the deprived communities become members of the core team. Forming a separate forum for women through mahila samooh (women's group) is a prerequisite for ensuring that in the tradition-bound rural milieu of Rajasthan, participation of girls in primary education becomes possible.

The main distinguishing feature of LJ is the bottom-up approach and the intensive mobilisation and support strategy at the village level. Through community involvement, with VEC playing a key role, the education system is made accountable to the community so that the community takes the responsibility for ensuring quality education for all school-going children. However, the development of VEC has been slow due to the fact that it needs total community participation and this needs time. In the context of the current move to transfer the responsibility for primary education to the panchayati raj bodies, LJ is now in the process of evolving norms for setting up VECs and formulating their responsibilities as education committees of Gram Panchayats. Some significant outcomes of Lok Jumbish during the last five years of its operation are as follows :

— there has been an impressive increase in enrolment-10 per cent per year for girls and 7 per cent for boys.

— an effective programme of NFE has been implemented-as many as 95 per cent of these centres are running efficiently and achieving equivalence with formal education.

Mobilising Women for Education

The National Policy on Education, 1986, was a landmark in the field of women's education, for it saw, empowerment of women as a critical precondition for their participation in the education process. To concretise this policy objective into an implementable strategy, the Mahila Samakhya Programme was designed to mobilise and organise women for education through creating an environment for learning.

The Mahila Samakhya programme, which is currently being implemented in seven states in the country (UP, AP, Gujarat, Karnataka, Bihar, Madhya Pradesh & Assam) and covers over 5000 villages, has been recognised as an effective and successful mobilisation strategy. The key elements of this programme relate both to a wider understanding and definition of education, as well as to strategies which emphasise processes rather than the mechanical fulfillment of set targets.

Mahila Samakhya understands "education" in the broadest sense of the term. Education is a continuous process to critically engage with one's environment and society, and to acquire the knowledge and skills to negotiate change from a position of strength. The principal strategy is to mobilise and organise women into collectives called 'mahila sanghas', providing them the space and gender sensitive inputs to reflect on their lives, to identify their needs and evolve collective ways of dealing with their problems. It is in this process, as women begin to question, analyse, learn new ways of thinking and doing, set their agendas for change, and make informed choices, that terms such as 'participation' and 'mobilising for education' gain new meaning. The experience of the programme over the past seven years has shown that the learning cycle invariably generates a demand for literacy, a demand which it must be emphasised is articulated by the women as a felt need.

The multi-dimensional aspects of education as life-skills, information, knowledge, and literacy, are all evident in the programme. Education as life skills connotes confidence and self esteem, at individual and collective levels, to affirm existence as an equal partner in society, a loss of fear, gaining recognition and respect within the family and the community, and ability to take decisions and act for change. This spiral of confidence and self esteem has enabled the women and 'sanghas' to effectively apply information and knowledge and competently chart and map new horizons for themselves in a variety of ways.

The diverse impact of this learning process is discernible in all the MS states. Women are addressing issues of access and improvement of civic amenities, problems of drinking water, wages, housing, ensuring education for girls, making schools and the health system more accountable, bravely confronting violence against women and social practices like child marriage and the devadasi system, confidently interacting and negotiating with power structures and are effectively participating in Panchayati Raj institutions. In all this, women are learning why problems exist, what are the obstacles-social and structural, which obstruct resolution of problems, from whom help can be sought and above all, the need for their own initiative to begin the process of initiating change. 'Sanghas' are now gradually moving from addressing livelihood issues to articulating their concerns on social practices which subordinate women.

While traversing the difficult path of addressing several of the above concerns, in several instances women have articulated a desire to acquire reading and writing skills. In most instances, feeling empowered, gaining knowledge, getting things done, have all been experienced without becoming literate. In some cases, the recognition of the need for literacy skills has come the hard way.

An innovative initiative in the area of girls/women's education has been the Mahila Shikshan Kendras. These are residential courses, aimed at developing a pool of aware, trained and literate women at the village level. As of date, there are 10 Mahila Shikshan Kendras in operation. While the direct impact of the MS educational strategy is yet to be fully felt, its impact is most visible in the confidence with which 'sanghas' are taking an active role in village education committees, making schools work, ensuring that the teachers come regularly and in many instances, ensuring that in their villages, children, particularly girl children, have access to formal education.

The efficacy of the Mahila Samakhya strategy of a long process of conscientisation was put to test with the announcement of statutory reservations for women in elections to Panchayat Raj institutions. Training and workshops were organised, information in an accessible manner was prepared and the interactive environment of the programme enabled a quick and wide dissemination of the new PR Act.

In Banda UP women trained as handpump meachanics became literate via the language of handpump maintenance. Region specific curricula have been developed around the concerns of women like violence, health and herbal medicine, wages, environment, forests among many others. Women have begun to effectively address the issues of the girl child education in addition to their own education. Sanghas are active partners in the diverse educational initiatives of the programme. The ECCE centres in Gujarat, the Bala Mitra Kendras/Jagjagi centers (NFE) for girls in Andhra Pradesh and Bihar, the Udan Khatolas in UP all provide a creative learning opportunity. Sanghas assist in selecting teachers, monitoring the centres, mobilising the community for education and in some cases (as in Andhra Pradesh) make some financial contribution as well. began to formalise their identity at the village level.

Yet another significant outcome of the programme has been the alternative streams that have emerged to address women's issues. A unique initiative has been the formation of Nari Adalats in Gujarat as an alternative forum of justice not only for women but for the community as well. Armed with a good knowledge of laws and procedures, women in Baroda began these as forums to address the cases of poor rural women who have been subjected to personal violence. As the Nari Adalats have gained in credibility and respect, a variety of cases ranging from abuse to land disputes are being brought for adjudication. In a completely different manner, the skilled women handpump mechanics and masons of Banda in UP have formed a cooperative, Vanangana, which not only imparts training to other women, but also takes over the maintenance of all handpumps in one block as well as several civil works in the area.

This has not been a linear process of learning and empowerment. There have been many crests and troughs, several steps backwards before a step could be taken forward. The zest and drive of the women has kept the programme vibrant. How will these learning processes be sustained in the long run? This is the challenge. Recognising that sanghas in isolation will not be able to survive, attempts are being made to build lateral solidarities among sanghas, and strengthening linkages with other groups and organisations, to enable women to consolidate their gains, continue to expand their universe of learning and work towards fashioning a gender-just society.

BEP was launched as a 'mission' programme in 1991 with the aid of UNICEF, Government of India and Government of Bihar. It is now in operation in 7 districts of Bihar. The main focus of BEP is universalisation of elementary education, particularly children in the 6-11 age group, with special emphasis on the girl child. Several new interventions have been made at the pre-primary, formal and non-formal education systems.

Universal access, universal participation and universal achievement are the three- pronged thrust areas of BEP. In order to make primacy education accessible, residential institutions like Aashram Shalas and low cost hostels have been set up in the remote areas. Shiksha Karmi centres have also been established so that the problem of teacher absenteeism does not arise. Local educated youth with no prior teaching experience are being trained to function as Shiksha Karmis. Consequently, there has been an increase in the number of school enrolment so much so that new schools have a double shift to accommodate all the students. The other objectives of BEP have been:

— drastic reduction in illiteracy, particularly in the 15-35 age group, bringing the literacy level in this age group at least to 80 per cent;

— modification in the educational system to serve the goal of equality of women and their empowerment; making necessary intervention to provide equal educational opportunities to adults and children belonging to the 'lower caste', ethnic minorities and the poorest sections of society;

— relating education to the working and living conditions of the people, improving thereby their ability to cope with the problems of livelihood, environment etc.; and

— laying special emphasis in all educational activities on science and environment and inculcation of a sense of social justice.

The critical aspect of BEP strategy is the active involvement of the community, the parents of the children attending the primary schools or NFE centres and adults who are expected to benefit from literacy programmes. In order to facilitate the participation of people at the grassroots level, the BEP has two people-based structures-the Village Education Committees (VECs) and the Mahila Samoohs.

The BEP conceptualises the VEC as a people's body, constituted by the villagers themselves and evolved through a process of self- determination. The VEC plays a critical role in the environment creation phase. The process of constituting VEC begins with the convening of the 'Aam Sabha' of the villagers. In this meeting of the villagers, detailed information about the BEP and its functions is given to the villagers. The members of the VEC are then chosen in the 'Aam Sabha'. VEC takes the full responsibility for the village school and its functioning. It is entrusted with the tasks of constructing and repairing the school building, and ensuring the enrolment and retention of children in the school, and attendance of teachers. It undertakes school mapping and micro-planning, providing an alternative to the top-down authoritarian management system. It also brings people together and creates a positive environment for education through prabhat-pheris, organisation of cultural and sports events. Hence the VEC is the cornerstone of BEP. Due representation is given to women and socially disadvantaged groups.

Teachers have been identified as the most important group who are instrumental in the development of a community network. A new teacher training strategy has emerged as a result of intensive participatory processes. The training is residential in nature, aims at renewal of teacher training practices and has a strong input of teacher motivation. The teachers are usually given total freedom to function. For instance, in Chaupatia block of West Champaran district, there has been a changed village environment, where the school and the community have come closer. The sole credit for all this goes to the teachers who enthusiatically participated in all the programmes of the BEP.

Women's empowerment and the equality of opportunities to the disadvantaged groups have been the mainstay of BEP. Efforts are made not only to provide opportunities, but also to create conditions whereby women can avail of them and articulate their demands. An extremely vibrant Mahila Samakhya programme is an integral component of the BEP which has been initiated in- over 1,680 villages, spread over 26 blocks.

The core objective of MS is to form strong, aware, active and responsible women's groups in the project villages called Mahila Samoohs. The entire 'Jagjagi' or the educational programme of the MS is an attempt to create an awareness amongst women and girls about the importance of education. Bal jag jagi centres have been formed for pre-primary or school preparedness programmes for pre-school children. The centres have a very positive impact on the village and their demand is increasing. Despite the fact that women find it difficult to acquire the necessary piece of land for the construction of 'kutir' where women's groups can hold their meetings, women's samoohs are determined to have a place of their own. 26 'kutirs' have been constructed so far by the samoohs. In the process of 'kutir' construction, the samoohs become stronger.

Besides the VECs and MS programme, village men and women also contribute in the mobilisation process as BEP functionaries. Shiksha Sathins go from village to village to encourage the villagers, particularly women and girls to participate in the educational programmes. Institutes of basic education like the primary schools, NFE centres, adult literacy centres, Jana Shikshan Nilayams (continuing education centres) are being made accountable to the village community. This mobilisation has been tremendous as many people have donated land for schools.

There are, however, some areas that need further strengthening. One of the problems in the composition of the VEC has been that at times VEC is constituted without a proper 'Aam Sabha' of the villagers. In such cases, it is not the villagers but the headmaster who chooses the members of the VEC. Obviously, a VEC constituted in this manner does not represent the villagers and is not likely to function effectively. Besides, it is necessary to strengthen the capacity of the VEC members and develop their skills in qualitative monitoring.

In the Jaipur village of Ranchi, Mahila Samooh constructed a Kutir for organising educational activities. A wealthy villager occupied their site and started building a house. The women protested along with a few concerned men of the village. But the men were arrested. The women got together and went to the police station and after much opposition and argument, prevailed upon the officer-in- charge. The officer-in-charge realised what the problem was. The men were then released and the wealthy landlord had to evacuate the site. This success of Mahila Samooh against stiff opposition increased their credibility and more women are now eager to join their group. It has also been observed that some of the mobilising strategies like rallies, bal melas, use of mass media (electronic as well as print) are mostly operational at the block level and their penetration at the village level has not been adequate. Considering the difficult socioeconomic conditions that prevail in Bihar, BEP has been working successfully and consistently to create a favourable environment for education of children and adults. A great deal still has to be achieved to ensure community mobilisation whereby women and the disadvantaged groups can participate without any social inhibitions.

NGO Initiatives

NGOs experiences in the field of basic education have

significantly influenced the design and the content of some of the EFA initiatives. NGOs have subsequently played a very significant role in providing a strong support structure to programme such as Shiksha Karmi, Lok Jumbish, BEP, DPEP etc. On their own too, they have worked out alternative and innovative approaches for providing basic education. Some of the areas in which they have made significant contribution include girls' and women's access to education, decentralised and participatory processes in planning and management, training of teachers and improving the quality and relevance of education, pedagogic and curriculum reform etc. The work of some of the NGOs is briefly described below.

Propel

This is an action research project for universalisation of elementary education that is undertaken by the Indian Institute of Education, Pune, Maharashtra state. The project perceives social and educational change as an integrated process in which the latent human energy necessary for propelling change and development is released through mutual understanding and collaboration between the government and the people. The project also affirms that essentially it is the people can bring about development and that the government and other agencies have to provide the necessary support and be facilitators. It has a three-fold approach to community mobilisation (i) increasing the community's access to necessary information (ii) building up its planning and action skills through participatory problem-solving (iii) ensuring that the community decisions regarding educational activities are respected and acted upon.

The basic assumption of the project is that in the final analysis, a community approach to educational development will have to be adopted and the local community will have to be made responsible for the proper education of all its members, that is children below six years of age (child care and pre-school education); children between 6-14 age group (primary education); young men and women in the age group 15-35 (non-formal education of youth and adults), with stress on the empowerment of girls and women in every aspect of the programme. All these programmes will have to be integrated with those of rural development. Within the framework of EFA, the project includes such mutually supportive programmes as early childhood care and education, women's empowerment, development orientation of youth, adult literacy, continuing education and recreational activities.

What propel has demonstrated is that in the matter of education for all, breaking the barrier of educational orthodoxy is a tough task, but that it can be tackled successfully if communities are mobilised and assisted to determine their own educational and development needs and priorities.

M Venkatarangaiya Foundation

Child labour continues to be a major factor in depriving children access to education. The MV Foundation has been working in Shankarpally Mandal, Andhra Pradesh, on the issue of elimination of child labour and universalisation of elementary education.

Every year, the organisation has been conducting mobilisation camps for children of bonded labour in order to withdraw them from work and admit them to appropriate levels in the schools. MV Foundation does not accept the widely held premise that children in poorer families go to work essentially to provide sustenance to the family. Their experience has shown that with a little motivation, even the children engaged in the most exploitative form of work can be withdrawn from work and admitted to schools. This is what MV Foundation has been demonstrating through its annual camps.

Another conclusion which MVF has arrived at through its experience is that children in the older age group will almost invariably drop out unless they are admitted to the class corresponding to their age.

The task of withdrawing children from work and their subsequent enrolment into formal schools is implemented with the active involvement of the youth clubs and the youth organisations, the gram panchayats and the elected representatives to the local bodies, and the parent-teacher's association attached to every village level government schools. Reaching out to the parents, children and employers through the local and already existing institutions is seen as a viable method to create a sustainable programme.

Social Welfare Research Centre

Rural working children need an educational process which is innovative in nature, so that their interests are sustained in attending school. Obviously, the timing of the school need to be considered to suit the needs of such children who come from families which cannot afford to send them to school during the day. The concept of night schools therefore becomes crucial for ensuring that the educational programme would reach out to such children. The Social Welfare Research Centre (SWRC), Tilonia, began such an experiment as far back as 1975 and the night school experiment has now been replicated by 11 organisations spread over 8 states. SWRC's approach to education, however, is different. The night schools are places of discovery for both the children and the teacher, the focus being on learning rather than on teaching. This project makes extensive use of creative visual media. The use of puppetry and street theatre to reach out to the masses has been a major means of communication employed by this project. The children are encouraged to conceptualise and perform street plays based on various issues. This has resulted in regular puppet show and street plays being staged in the villages, which have ensured a high level of people's participation and interest. In all the schools that have started functioning, VECs have been formed which look after the day to day running of these schools.

Butterflies is a programme of street and working children that has been operating in Delhi since 1988. It aims to empower street children with the knowledge and necessary skills necessary to protect their rights as children and provide them the necessary support and assistance for reinstatement with their families, where possible, and help them develop as respected and productive citizens. Butterflies focuses on using, the Convention on the Rights of the Child as a major tool for ensuring government and public accountability towards the well-being of all vulnerable children. It organises support services in the fulfillment of the street children's basic needs such as non-formal education, health care and recreation. It also organises children for collective action and networks with like-minded organisations concerned with Social Development and Children's Rights.

Eklavya

Founded in 1982, Eklavya is operating in several districts of Madhya Pradesh. Education for Eklavya centres around the needs and thought process of the child which involves joyful learning. Eklavya has evolved innovative curriculum, teaching methodology, and educational materials for teaching of science and social science to students of standards VI, VII and VIII. An innovative primary school programme (classes I to V) commenced from 1987. Science popularisation and environment activities are also undertaken.

Eklavya attempts to make a "significant change in the quality of teaching materials, teacher training and evaluation, creating awareness, motivation amongst administrators, teachers, parents and the public in general to change the quality of education available to children". The aim is to "create a situation in which children can be more active participative, intellectually stimulated and creative". Active participation of teachers, children and other resource person is always sought when the programmes are formulated. Eklavya also evolves subsidiary activities outside the school structures in order to create a suitable social and intellectual environment in which innovations can flourish. Educational innovation also involves the changing of administrative structure at the macro level so that it can be made more responsive to the growing needs.

Challenges of Implementing EFA

The recent initiatives in social and political mobilisation and the move towards decentralisation have to be understood against the complexities that characterise the Indian polity. Despite its federal nature, the Constitution of India gave greater power and authority to the central government than to the state governments. The setting up of the Planning Commission at the national level further exacerbated the centralising nature of the planning process.

Thus, the district and lower level units were assigned the responsibility of implementing the plans prepared and approved at the state and national levels. Education in the Constitution was made a state subject and remained so until 1976 when, with the 42nd Amendment, it was placed in the Concurrent List. The purpose of doing so was to bring about some degree of uniformity and comparability across the states in the field of education. The concept of concurrency was given an operational meaning by the National Policy on Education.

The Policy envisaged concurrency as a 'meaningful partnership between the centre and the states.' In reality, this has not necessarily happened. For India is a multiparty democracy and while for a long time after independence, the party in power at the centre was also in power at the state levels, this has changed in recent years so that in a large number of states the political parties in power at the state level often reflect regional aspirations of the people.

As a result, polarisation of political power has often crystallised in a different direction. Even with regard to the 73rd and 74th Amendment to the Constitution which provide enough scope for involvement of local bodies in education, it needs to be mentioned that these amendments are in the nature of 'enabling legislation' for creating these bodies at the local levels and defining the extent of their authority. The states are obliged to set up these institutions and delegate to them powers and financial resources which they consider appropriate and necessary. However, in the prevalent system of political pluralism, doubts can be raised whether the state-level leadership would be willing to share powers with the local leadership.

It is important to take note of these complexities that characterise the Indian democratic system for the very same factors noted above could either slow down or provide a tremendous fillip to the mass education of children and adults. While the recent EFA initiatives show that the strategies of political and social mobilisation are beginning to show positive results, India still has a long way to go and there is certainly no room for complacency at this stage. Some of the unfinished tasks that need attention are the following.

The biggest challenge before the EFA initiatives is how to sustain the motivation and the interest of the community so that their sense of control and ownership of the programme begins to increase. Participation in its various dimensions, has to be, recognised as a basic principle of action, an overall development strategy. A participatory culture can only grow and sustain in an environment which genuinely recognises its value. If such an environment does not exist, then the danger of bureaucratisation of the programme is very real. Overzealous officials can often enforce participation through administrative fiats. As a result, a programme can very soon lose its vitality, vigour and its momentum. This is not to suggest that the bureaucracy has no role to play. Rather, the bureaucracy has to work by forging alliances with a variety of institutions, organisations, groups and people so that their active involvement in promoting and supporting EFA initiatives, is ensured. Sustaining community involvement for primary education also has another dimension. Because of the longer time duration involved, it will have to be sustained through certain institutionalised structures such as Parent-Teacher Associations, VECs and PRIs.

A related issue is that of community ownership of the programme. This can happen if the community is involved in the programme from its very beginning, is actively involved in the decision-making process and has a certain degree of financial autonomy. Likewise, in the case of an educational intervention, phasing out of the outside group/ agency has to be planned, worked out and suitably implemented. The experience of some of the

EFA initiatives is showing that the strategy for 'phasing out' should not be hastened but should also not be postponed indefinitely. There is also a great need for capacity-building at the local level and for local level organisations such as the VECs (village education committees) to evolve rather than to be constituted from above, in which case, they tend to be dysfunctional, ineffective and may exist only on paper.

The contention that rural communities are cohesive, homogenous and that they work in the larger interest of their people, is erroneous. There are divisions not only on the basis of economic and political interests, but the divide on the basis of caste, class, religion, gender, is often very sharp. The areas of conflict heighten with the introduction of direct elections. Therefore, the implicit faith that the PRIs (Panchayati Raj Institutions) would necessarily work in the interests of the community, needs to be tempered by regarding them from a more pragmatic viewpoint in which strife, conflict of interests, shifting loyalties and alignments, would be recognised. In such situations, the kinds of safeguards that need to be taken and the counterveiling forces that would make the PRIs accountable to the interests of the community, need to be considered.

While the recent EFA initiatives show that the strategies of political and social mobilising are beginning to show positive results, India still has a long way to go and there is certainly no room for complacency at this stage.

The EFA initiatives have created new structures such as autonomous organisations at the state and district levels. Very often, these organisations are headed by individuals who were not actively involved with the programme at the planning stage. Frequent change of personnel at the centre and state levels makes the programme routine at an early stage. Therefore, there is a need for continuous orientation and interaction with the personnel who are involved in programme planning and implementation at all levels. Even VEC members would need suitable orientation to enable them to play their role in a more meaningful and dynamic manner.

The EFA initiatives have created new or alternate management structures because the existing structures were found to be ineffective, inflexible, hierarchical. The question that needs to be constantly asked is whether the alternate structures have imbibed the new ethos, the new management practices. Are efforts continuously made to infuse dynamism in the new system so as to prevent regression to the old habits and routines? These questions are important for the danger of reverting back to the old structures and to the earlier practices and work styles, is very real.

In the case of centrally-sponsored schemes, the role of the central and state governments in facilitating decentralised planning has to be clearly delineated. While the role of the central government might be active and direct in the initial stages, it would have to be facilitative and enabling thereafter so as to promote local initiatives and decentralisation. This could be done through strengthening planning capacities at the state and district levels. Microplanning activities which have been initiated in many districts attempt to ensure critical and sustained involvement of the community in educational planning processes at the village level. It would be necessary to institutionalise local level planning competencies as a long-term strategy.

Some of the EFA initiatives have shown that concerted efforts are made to focus on gender issues. In a society in which patriarchal norms militate against participation of girls and women in the educational programmes, such a thrust is absolutely necessary. Or else the danger is that the gender issues can get marginalised or regarded only as a women's concern. Some of the EFA initiatives that have responded to community needs, have resulted in innovative responses such as setting up creches (Udān Khatolas), non-formal education centres, day- time/night-time non-formal education centres, residential hostels, etc.

If different sections of the society have to be mobilised around EFA, it must be brought to the centre of national attention. National leaders, as well as political leaders at all levels would have to take the lead in the nationwide dialogue in order to build public awareness and understanding, leading to support and involvement of the whole society. Participation and mobilisation on an ongoing basis can only be promoted on the foundation of a national consensus on the major goals and priorities, and the main strategies for achieving them. A process of consensus-building that is an on-going process would need to be initiated. The mass media could play a very dynamic role in facilitating this process. Such a process of building a national consensus could be non-partisan so that it could survive change of government and of personalities in high places.

These are some of the unfinished tasks that have now become major challenges as India further strengthens, consolidates and expands EFA initiatives by launching the National Elementary Mission (NEEM) as well as initiates a new collaborative effort between the Government of India and the UN System Support for Community-Based Primary Education. This is a joint effort of the Government of India and five UN agencies namely UNICEF, UNDP, ILO, UNESCO and UNFPA to provide programme support in a coordinated manner to on-going efforts of Government of India towards the goal of universalisation of elementary education.

7

Policy Framework for Educational Development

In this chapter we shall discuss a few programmes of high priority which will have to be developed over the next ten years or so to provide good education for all our people and to create a national system of education which will meet the needs and aspirations of the people.

Adult Education Development

Significance and Priority. We shall begin this discussion with adult education because we attach the highest significance to this programme. We believe that illiteracy and lack of 'proper' adult education is a serious impediment. not only to the growth of the individuals concerned but to the socioeconomic development of the country as a whole. We also believe that any investment in adult education, especially of the illiterate poor, will yield quick results in terms of socioeconomic progress and will be extremely rewarding in proportion to its quantum. It is also our considered view that a massive programme of adult education should have been developed on a priority basis as soon as we became free and that illiteracy should have been liquidated within a few years of independence. But this priority was unfortunately not adopted. The Constitution gave the franchise to all adults, but it made no provision for adult education which would have made it more meaningful. On the other hand, it adopted the traditional view that we should provide universal elementary education for children in a short period (1950-60) and that the problem of adult education would solve itself over the years. This has led to a neglect of adult education in the post-independence period; and as the implementation of the programme of elementary education itself has been delayed, we have really missed the bus. The percentage of literacy increased from about 14 in 1947 to only about 30 in 1971. What is even worse, the people have not been strengthened and organised to participate in development so that national development itself has received a great set-back. It is high time that these wrong policies were abandoned. We must realise that the programme of educating and organising the people to create a new social order cannot be implemented except through adult education.

Objectives and Content

We believe the initiative in the creation of the new egalitarian social order will have to be taken by the poor and oppressed people themselves. They can effectively do so if they are made aware of their innate strengths and of the exploitative social reality around them, if they are actively involved in socially productive useful work (i.e., are guaranteed useful employment), if they are assisted to create institutions which can give them a sense of self-reliance and a capacity to raise their standards of living, and if they are fearless and organised to resist all exploitation effectively. The object of adult education of the poor, therefore, can only be to awaken the 'I' and the 'us' in them so that they can assert themselves, both individually and collectively, and to enable them to perceive that they can be free from fear, want, and dependency. We must especially guard against the danger, ever present, that adult education may be used as a tool for educating the poor to their present marginal status, conformity and resignation or for encouraging escapist trends. This does not mean direct political mobilisation which is a task for political parties. But it does mean that the education of the poor must have an essential political component to enable them to come into their own.

The content of adult education of the common people who are mostly illiterate should ordinarily include literacy which is an essential prerequisite for autonomous access to the growing knowledge in the world. But it need not be overemphasized. A literate adult who has a closed mind and does not use his literacy. For continuously adding to his knowledge is no better than an illiterate. It is also necessary to emphasize that the best learning takes place, not in school, but in work and life situations, that learning, working, and living are inseparable, and that each of these acquires a meaning only when fully correlated with the others. This is especially true of adults so that a literacy programme unrelated to the working and living conditions of the learners or to the challenges of the environment and the developmental needs of the country is not likely to enthuse or lead to any meaningful individual or social gains. While emphasizing the acquisition of literacy skills by the illiterate people, therefore, a programme of adult education must also have a broader content of education relevant to the environment and to the immediate felt needs of the learners and the challenges of improving their own socio-economic status and national development in which they must themselves participate with conviction and enthusiasm. In particular, such a programme should contain an 'appropriate mix' of the following themes suited to the needs of different individuals and groups:

(1) Development of vocational skills to improve earning capacity.

(2) General Education (including health education and family planning).

(3) Citizenship education (including essential political education).

(4) Development studies or a knowledge of the developmental problems of the country in which their own problems are rooted, the role of the people in the solution of these problems and their actual involvement in social and developmental programmes.

(5) Physical education, games and sports, recreation. and participative cultural activities.

The programme should also be extremely flexible with regard to duration, time, location or instructional arrangements and should be as diversified as the needs and capacities of the individuals or groups participating in the programmes. Consequently, the planning of the exact content of the curricula needed by specific individuals or groups can never be done centrally. They would have to be intensively local and dialogic in the sense that they should be evolved, in a highly decentralised fashion, by the local worker in discussion with the adults with whom he is working. All that a central organisation can and should do is (1) to create a cadre of good and sensitised workers, (2) to provide them with good training in social objectives, curricular construction, and appropriate methods of teaching and evaluation, and (3) to put out a large variety of well-prepared and tested teaching and learning material from which each worker can choose what suits his requirements best. The critical significance of these central roles is obvious.

Motivation: Adults cannot be made a captive audience and have to be motivated to learn. This will be possible only to the extent they perceive that the programmes offered are of use to them. The best motivation is seen where an attempt is made to create awareness or when the programmes involve them in the solution of their day-to-day problems and strive to bring about some improvement in their life, however small. Good workers who have established a rapport with the people, a well-organised programme which fits the needs and interests of the learners, and good methods of teaching which make learning a joyful, cooperative enterprise between the teacher and students, will be of great help. It will also be of advantage if adult education can be made an integral part of a development programme or a social movement.

Organisation: Perhaps the most difficult and complex issues about adult education relate to organisation: motivating adults, selection and training of workers, production of teaching and learning materials, and, above all, the actual development of this massive programme on the ground. The problem assumes greater significance because it cannot be solved by money alone. There is enough experience to show that, if money is poured into the scheme without the other essential inputs or adequate preparation, we will only end up with corruption and bogus statistics. The non-monetary inputs are, therefore, crucial, not only to save money which is certainly not overabundant, but to save the movement itself. Yet another factor which deserves serious attention is that the adult education, movement can also be used to stimulate the young to national service and to channelise their energies and idealism in fruitful directions and thus make them development-oriented. It would be almost criminal not to explore and exploit the fullest potential of this possibility.

In the light of past experience, we find that three alternative approaches are possible. If quality is the main objective and not numbers, the movement may be organised on a selective basis, by giving full encouragement and providing the needed facilities and financial support in ail cases where one finds dedicated and competent workers or adults desiring to learn. Alternatively, quality can still be maintained and numbers can be increased to some extent, if it is organised as a mass campaign in a small selected area(s) where conditions are favourable. While both these methods are important and should be widely used in the early stages of the campaign, our ultimate objective should be to adopt the third approach and to develop programmes of adult education as a nation-wide movement of good quality. This is the most difficult challenge and will demand supreme skills of organisation, as a mass movement and a massive involvement of all agencies and individuals capable of participating therein.

To what extent can we use the teachers and students in the existing formal system for promoting literacy and adult education? The potential of the proposal is obviously immense because there are nearly 16 million students and nearly four million teachers and administrators who can be used as workers for this programme. One view is that the inertia and inefficiency of the system and the class orientation of the teachers and students will make it impossible to work out the scheme in its proper perspective. Another view is that it would be wrong to ignore the formal system altogether, especially because the development of this programme can be an instrument to start the process of transformation within the formal system itself.

Moreover, it may be contended that a massive programme of adult education cannot be developed without fully exploiting the large intra-structure of the formal system. We do not, therefore, think that this is an 'either-or' issue. We must involve students, teachers, and institutions within the formal system of education on a selective and increasing basis. Any voluntary initiative shown in this programme by individual schools or groups of teachers and students should receive due recognition and support.

There should also be adequate incentives for individual educational institutions to participate in the programme by linking such participation to developmental grants for buildings, libraries, laboratories, etc.; and it should be possible for students to participate in the scheme and to earn a part of their maintenance costs. Even the possibility of making participation in the programme obligatory for all teachers and students should be explored; and a beginning in this direction can certainly be made by individual educational institutions committed to the programme.

At the same time, we must realise that there are definite advantages in beginning this programme in a big way outside the formal educational system by utilising the large teaching resources, both individual and institutional, which are available in the society and which, though largely unused or underutilised at present, can be harnessed for the programmes. For instance, village panchayats, cooperative societies, youth clubs, mahila mandals, etc., can play useful roles; and large numbers of educated persons who are not professional teachers but who have the necessary enthusiasm and commitment could be selected and trained to organise literacy and other adult education programmes.

All things considered, it appears that we are more likely to obtain the best results only if we combine the various approaches and techniques suitably. The backdrop of a mass movement is in any case inescapable.

But against it, we may combine the selective and mass campaign approaches. The workers can be selected, on a large scale, from both among the teachers and the students within the system as well as from the stock of enthusiastic and committed individuals outside the education system, and especially from among the poor people themselves. If anything, the latter may prove to be the better and larger source for the supply of key workers.

In the development of this programme, voluntary organisations will have a significant role to play. Drawing upon non-formal resources of society will call for more, not less, organisational effort on the part of government. There should be special schemes to assist them and an adequate organisational effort to harness their services. Institutions known for their competence and commitment should be given a large measure of autonomy to innovate and experiment. Similarly, industry and other employers of labour should be under legal obligation to make their employees literate and, where necessary, certain forms of assistance (such as training of workers) may be made available to them. Literacy and adult education programmes should also be organised for all illiterate workers employed on government projects and development works.

Out-of-school Youth (Age Group 15-21)

What has been said above about the education of adults will also apply, mutatis mutandis, to the education of out-of-school youth (age-group 15-21) which, in our opinion, is the second major programme for the education of the people. The significance of this group is immense (it is about 85 per cent of the total population of this age) and investment in its education will obviously pay rich and early dividends. The motivation of this group is stronger and its educability greater. As peer group learning is very significant, we can effectively use students as well as persons selected and trained from among the group itself, for the development of the programme. Vocational education has a special import for this group most of whom will be looking for a career. We will also have to provide adequate opportunities for continuing formal education, interrupted for various reasons, to all those who desire to improve their career prospects through such education.

Programmes of adult education, whether for out-of-school youth (age-group 15-21) or for adults (age 21 and over), will need the production of a large volume of imaginatively planned teaching and learning materials of the best quality, not only for literacy work but also for post-literacy and follow-up work with the neo-literates. A wide network of libraries and reading-rooms will also have to be organised for the purpose. Effective use may also be made of posters and wall-papers. The universities will have to play an important role in generating materials, conducting research, evaluation, and training of workers. The mass media, such as the press and radio, can play a major role in the promotion of the massive programmes of adult education we have in view and should be fully utilised. The development of the programme in rural areas and for women will need special efforts and emphasis. Needless to say, it will also be necessary to organise a massive programme for the training of workers and to develop a good system of - supervision, evaluation, and continuous monitoring. The programme will have to be launched immediately and will have to be kept up at a very high pitch for about ten years.

Universal Elementary Education

We shall now turn to the discussion of the third

programme for the education of the people, viz., the provision of universal elementary education for children in the age-group (6-14) with which we shall link the problem of pre-school education also.

Past achievements and failures: While we have travelled far ahead of our position in 1947, the remaining journey to the destination visualised in Article 45 of the Constitution is very long and difficult. This will be clear from our achievements in the four specific goals of the programme, viz., (a) universal provision of facilities, (b) universal enrolment, (c) universal retention, and (d) improvement of standards.

(1) The first step in the programme is to provide an elementary school within easy reach of every child. So far we have been able to provide a primary school within walking distance from the home of most children in the age-group 6-11 and a similar facility at the middle school stage is available for about 60 per cent of the children in the age-group 11-14. It will, therefore, be possible to realise the goal of universal provision of schooling facilities, i.e., providing a primary and middle school within walking distance from the home of every child within a few years and without much difficulty.

(2) The next step is to ensure that every child is enrolled in a school. The enrolments in 1975-76 in classes IN stood at 66.5 million and those in classes VI-VIII, at 16.5 million. These figures, however, conceal a good deal of bogus enrolment which is proportionately greater in the more backward-States. If universal enrolment in the agegroup 6-14 is to be reached within ten years, i.e., by 1985-86, these enrolments will have to increase to 85 million and 50 million respectively. in other words, there would have to be an additional enrolment of 52 million in about ten years or about 52 lakhs per

year as against an average of about 24 lakhs a year achieved in the past 30 years. This, in itself, is difficult; and it becomes all the more so because the children who are now out of school consist mostly of the hard core of non-attendants, viz., girls and children from scheduled castes, scheduled tribes and other weaker sections. Unless a major effort is made, it will not be possible to reach the goal of universal enrolment.

(3) The third step in the programme is to ensure that there is universal retention, i.e., no child once enrolled in school drops out till he completes the elementary course or reaches the age of 14 years. Unfortunately, a great weakness of the present programme is that there is a large proportion of drop-outs or push-outs, due partly to the irrelevance and poor quality of education, but mainly to the insistence on full-time attendance which is not possible for children of poor families who are required to work. There is clear evidence to show that the proportion of such drop-outs (or wastage) between classes IN and classes I-VIII is very high (about 60 per cent and 75 per cent respectively) and has remained almost unchanged during the past 30 years. The problem of universal retention is, therefore, even more difficult to be solved.

4) Side by side these programmes of expansion, steps have also to be taken to improve the quality of education because Article 45 implies both a quantitative and a qualitative target. Unfortunately, our failure in this regard is also dismal because standards of elementary education have continued to be unsatisfactory. This is probably the most difficult aspects of the task and will need the most intensive and sustained efforts.

A new strategy: The reasons for this failure are both social and educational. There has been a lack of political commitment and the programme has never received adequate priority and resources. Raising the standards of living, over-all development, massive campaigns of adult education, and active involvement of the people are all absolutely essential for its success. But none of these have been given due attention. Programmes of this type have also to be implemented quickly as crash programmes, say, in a period of 5-10 years. But we have made them long-term affairs which have only made the problem more difficult through increase of population, rise in unit costs, and slowing down of the tempo. The content of education has been largely irrelevant and the quality of education, poor. Consequently, the attracting and holding power of the schools has been very low. Above all, the greatest handicap has been the formal system of education which we have adopted: it increases costs through its insistence on the exclusive employment of full-time teachers, keeps millions of children out by its insistence of full-time attendance, and converts the bulk of the children from poor families who are required to work into dropouts or push-outs.

We should learn from these lessons of history and adopt a new strategy to make a success of this programme in the years ahead. Some of its major aspects are given below:

(1) The problem should be solved in a short-term plan of ten years at the most.

(2) At present, we operate on the basis of a system of single-point entry and make fresh enrolments in class I only (at about the age of six years), and expect these children to rise up to the next higher class each year and to remain in school till they complete the elementary school or the age of 14 years. This slows down the progress very greatly,

especially because of the large prevalence of drop-outs. We should give up this outmoded system which does not suit our needs. Instead, we should adopt a multi-point entry and an elastic system of promotions so that even older children who are out of school can be brought simultaneously under instruction. Similarly, we should give up our insistence on full-time education and part-time education should be made available to all children who are required to work and cannot attend school on a whole-time basis. In other words, while the existing stream of full-time education which admits children in Grade I at about the age of six, and takes them up sequentially to class VIII at about the age of 14 plus, should continue. But it should not be the only stream of providing elementary education to children and should be supplemented by three other parallel streams to suit the needs of different categories of children. These will include: (a) part-time education to children in the age-group 6-11 who cannot go to school on a whole-time basis in order to enable them to become functionally literate or to complete class V; (b) part-time education for children in the age-group 11-14 who have never been to school, or dropped out very early, in order to enable them to become functionally literate or complete class V; and (c) part-time continuation education in classes VI-VIII for all children who have completed class V, either on a full-time or on a part-time basis, but who cannot continue to study further on a whole-time basis. These four different streams, taken together, will meet the educational needs of all children in the age-group of 6-14 and bring them under instruction. They will also solve the problem of non-enrolment or drop-outs and ensure that all children in the age-group 6-14 shall remain under instruction, on a full-time basis if possible, and on a part-time basis if necessary. It is also necessary to emphasize that, for the programmes of part-time education, we need not depend upon full-time professional teachers alone. The large unutilised teaching resources in the community should be mobilised here also as in adult education.

(3) Special attention should be paid to the education of girls and of the children of scheduled castes, scheduled tribes, and other weaker sections of the society.

(4) The massive adult education campaigns recommended earlier can be a great asset to this programme because the education of the parents is the best guarantee for enrolling and retaining children in schools. Further motivational and economic support for the programme would be obtained if simultaneous efforts are made to improve the standards of living of the common people.

(5) It must be realised that the programme can be handled successfully only on the basis of decentralisation. In the last analysis, this programme involves the planning of the education of each individual child and the planning of education of every community. This implies a highly decentralised and yet effective administration far in advance of anything we have attempted so far. A large variety of models is available for the purpose and we may also design our own new models. What is needed is a good deal of innovation, commitment, courage, and firm decisions.

(6) One of the principal reasons which has hindered the progress of universal elementary education is

the paucity of financial resources. If this is to be overcome, the unit cost of educating a child at the elementary stage should be kept within reasonable limits through such measures as modification of the wage-structure, adoption of part-time education, and increasing pupil-teacher ratio, preferably through the use of the double-shift system. What is even more important, we must plug the several loopholes in the existing. system which lead to tremendous waste. Simultaneously, we should accord higher priority to the programme so that it gets larger resources, both in absolute terms and in proportion.

(7) The States such as Bihar, Madhya Pradesh, Orissa, and Rajasthan present a difficult problem. They have large populations of scheduled castes and tribes. There are strong prejudices against the education of girls. The number of non-attending children they have is proportionately larger while the overall resources available to them are much smaller. Unless special efforts are made and special financial assistance is given by the Centre, they will not be able to tackle this huge problem satisfactorily. Each State will have to make similar special efforts for its own less developed or backward areas.

Content and Quality

The content and quality of elementary education and its universalisation are interdependent. If the content of education is relevant and its quality good, the attracting and holding power of the schools increases and this helps in universalisation itself. Without this support from within the school system, no external effort can ever succeed. Even if it were to succeed, there is hardly any point in universalising bad education.

The basic reform in the content of elementary education is to introduce productive work and social service activities as integral elements of the educational process. This will bring the hand and the brain together and also emphasize social rather than the individual objectives of education. Mahatma Gandhi was absolutely correct when he insisted on this reform as basic to the transformation of the educational system from its middle class to mass orientation. But the introduction of this reform is far from easy. It is not merely a question of training teachers or providing equipment. It is also a basic issue of changing social values and it will not be possible to implement this programme within the school unless we also make a simultaneous effort to make work and social service respected in the wider society itself. It must be emphasized, however, that this reform is meant mainly for the upper and middle classes who have education but do not work with their hands and who consider work-experience or social service as an irrelevant waste of time for their children. Its counterpart for the children of the poor who work with their hands but receive no education is part-time education. We need, therefore, not only the introduction of work in formal full-time education but a large-scale adoption of the system of part-time instruction which will build education round work.

The other major change needed in the curriculum at the elementary stage is to link it closely with the local environment and to make it relevant in itself and not merely a preparation for the secondary school. At present, we have a system of centralised curriculum-construction: the best curricula are supposed to be prepared at the national level and handed down to the States; and each State insists on having a common curriculum for all the schools in its area. Such a centrally planned curriculum cannot provide for local variations and often becomes irrelevant and inert to the learners. Similarly, the curricula at the elementary stage are generally designed to prepare the student for the secondary stage and hence they become irrelevant to the needs of the learners, and especially to the later life of the children, if they do not continue their studies beyond elementary education. If such situations are to be avoided, we must plan the content of education very differently. It should be planned as an end in itself and to suit the local environment, as a result of a continuing dialogue between the teachers and learners. Needless to say, such curricula will vary from area to area, and even in the same area, from situation to situation. What we have to do, therefore, is to decentralise the curriculum-making process and hand down, not ready-made curricula, but the skills of curriculum-construction to all elementary school teachers.

The Common School As was pointed out earlier, our inegalitarian society has created an inegalitarian system of education which segregates the rich and well-to-do from the poor, the children of the rich and well-to-do attend the minority of 'good' schools which include all prestigious institutions, public schools, English-medium schools, and quality institutions while the common people have access mostly to the government-supported schools which are generally of poor quality. This segregation must end immediately throughout the educational system. But probably the most urgent step needed is to end it at the elementary stage so that all children, in the impressionable age-group 6-14, rub. shoulders with each other, irrespective of social class or caste, and learn and work together. This would be a very effective method of promoting equality, social cohesion, and national integration. We are, therefore, strongly of the view that the common school system must be adopted immediately at the elementary stage. This is basically an urban issue; and strongest opposition to the proposal comes from the top vested interests who use the best schools to perpetuate their privileged position. Only firm political action can break it.

PRE-SCHOOL EDUCATION

Another major reform is to extend the pre-school education, which is now an almost exclusive monopoly of the urban and well-to-do classes, to the rural areas and the poor people. This cannot be done on the basis of traditional models which are very costly. What we need is innovative and low-cost methods that can be multiplied within the available resources. Among these, the following may be mentioned:

(1) In Maharashtra, the training of primary and pre-school teachers has been integrated. This makes two major reforms possible: (a) The play-way methods of teaching can be introduced in classes I and II where they are badly needed and where they help in reducing wastage; and (b) the primary teachers can run, as part of their duty, children's play-centres attached to primary schools (especially in all cases where the instructional hours are reduced to three or four per day) and thus provide some pre-school education to large numbers of children with only a marginal addition to costs.

(2) The Tamil Nadu experiment of using locally available educated women to run pre-schools reduces the cost per child per year very greatly and deserves adoption everywhere.

(3) Child-care can be an important theme round which adult education of women can be built. This will help in improving the home-background of pre-school children and assist in their socialisation on right lines.

(4) Large numbers of women are employed in the organised sector and on several programmes of development undertaken by official and non-official agencies. Arrangements should be made for the care and education of their young children. The excellent work done by the mobile creche movement developed by the late Shrimati Meera Mahadevan is a good model in this regard.

(5) Above all, it must be remembered that any attempt to draw a rigid demarcation between school and pre-school years will come in the way of universalising elementary education itself. Our primary schools have no pre-schools or creches attached to them. The most common work which girls from poor families are required to do is to look after young children. On the one hand, we are anxious to promote girls' education and organise a number of programmes to increase their enrolment. On the other, we do not permit girls to bring young children with them and request them to leave them at home before coming to school. Since this is impossible, in practice it means only one thing: the girls are prevented from joining schools and there is a positive disincentive in the system against the spread of education among girls from poor families. Experiments have been tried, notably by the late Shrimati Tarabai Modak, wherein. small creches or preschools were attached to primary schools and were conducted by girls themselves under the general supervision of the teachers. The additional costs involved in the programme were marginal, but they succeeded very well in enrolling a large number of girls from the poor families. This idea can and should be adopted on a mass scale.

Mass Movement for Educational Development

Before closing this discussion, we would like to emphasize a point of supreme significance, viz., none of the three programmes of people's education referred to here (adult education, education of out-of-school youth, and universal elementary education) can succeed unless a powerful, nation-wide movement is organised for the purpose and unless a simultaneous effort is made to organise the poor people and to improve their standard of living. This is essentially a package deal and without it we will not be able to meet the requirements implicit in these programmes such as,

— motivating millions of illiterate adults and youth to learn and to acquire literacy;

— changing the motivation of millions of parents and drawing millions of non-attending children into schools and retaining them therein;

— transforming the present orientations of teachers, generally geared to the classes and to the middle class white collar attitudes and changing their values almost overnight, into work and development-oriented ones geared to the service of the common people;

— training of thousands of non-teachers and enthusing them to participate in the programmes and utilising all social institutions also for the purpose;

— organising a big programme of non-formal education outside the school system; and

— taking vigorious steps to transform the existing formal system radically and creating and maintaining a climate of sustained and dedicated hard work, both within and without the school system.

We should also emphasize that even the purely educational tasks, apart from the political and economic tasks of organising the poor and raising their standards of living, are beyond the capacity of teachers as a profession, beyond the resources of the school system itself, and beyond even the best efforts of the entire bureaucratic machine. These tasks can be performed only through a nation-wide social movement in which all the people are intensely involved. It is the responsibility of all the public leadership, and especially of the political leadership, to organise and sustain such a movement at a high level of tempo over the next ten years or so and the duty of the bureaucracy, the teaching community,and all educated persons to support these efforts.

Access to Education

There has been a very rapid and unplanned expansion of secondary and higher education during the. past thirty years, not necessarily for good academic or developmental reasons. Some of the demand arises from wrong employment policies wherein a university degree becomes necessary even for jobs where it is irrelevant. A boy often goes to college because he does not get a job when he completes secondary education and a girl does so while she is waiting to be married.

Secondary schools and colleges have becomes status symbols and are often started for the political and economic advantages they confer on their entrepreneurs, without any attention to proper planning of locations, academic viability, or level of unit costs. There is also a built-in element of expansion within the system itself: pressures from the educated unemployed lead to expansion of secondary schools and colleges which, in their turn, lead to greater unemployment and more intensive pressures. We have also refused to adopt selective admissions and preferred to follow an open-door policy in practice, if not always in theory. Since the available resources in men and money are limited; we create a dual system at these stages to meet the challenges of expansion.

There is a core of prestigious and good quality institutions (i.e., institutions in which education is closely linked to good employment) where admissions are selective (and often highly so) and where students are selected on merit which, in practice, implies their ability to choose their parents carefully! This is surrounded by a large penumbra of poor quality institutions, mostly of general education, wherein the so-called open-door access only guarantees that the child of the common man shall have admission in some institution, however poor, and in some cases, however useless. Ironically enough, this policy of open-door admissions which was supposed to be formulated in the interests of the poor and is strongly defended by them in the name of vertical mobility, mainly benefits the upper and middle classes in practice, and particularly those who live in places where institutions of secondary and higher education are located.

Most children from the underprivileged social groups are eliminated, on harsh economic grounds, at the elementary stage itself; mediocre and third-rate children of the upper and middle classes find easy access to the system especially in -urban areas; and even the talented children of the poor, who are a national asset, often remain outside the system. The direct and indirect subsidies given at these stages mostly go to the upper and middle classes; and the system tends to reproduce an exploiting and parasitic class rather than individuals who will serve the common people. It is these inequalities, inadequacies and weaknesses of the system that we must strive to eliminate or reduce.

General Policy

In the present situation when we are not able to provide even elementary education, post-elementary education cannot be claimed as a matter of right. The policy with regard to its provision should, therefore, be governed by the following principles:

(1) Expansion of facilities in post-elementary education should be closely related to the resources available and the maintenance of proper standards.

(2) A distinction should be made between an individual's right to lifelong learning and the payment of a subsidy from the public treasury for the post-elementary education of an individual. The former is a fundamental human right and no State should have the authority to tell an individual to study thus far and no further. But the State subsidies for post-elementary education should be available, in view of the financial constraints, only to the deserving and economically handicapped persons.

(3) In view of the high priority given to adult and universal elementary education, the resources available for all post-elementary education would be comparatively limited. These should, therefore, be used with the greatest economy and effectiveness, especially in programmes which serve the common people (such as the identification and cultivation of talent from among the poor people) and in qualitative improvement (which is urgent and hitherto neglected).

(4) The bulk of subsidies now provided in post-elementary education, which mostly go to upper and middle classes should be reduced progressively while those meant for the underprivileged groups should be increased.

(5) Even while it is necessary to regulate the over-all enrolments in post-elementary education on grounds of the large and rapidly increasing numbers of the educated unemployed, the access of the underprivileged groups to post-elementary education should be increased so that the new policy of regulated enrolments may result only in limiting the access of the upper and middle classes to secondary and higher education to reasonable proportions.

In order to increase the access of the underprivileged social groups to secondary and higher education, it is suggested that the type of assistance, which is now provided to scheduled caste and scheduled tribe students at these stages, should be extended to all children and youth from families with an income below a prescribed level, irrespective of caste, religion, or sex. In particular, the following measures are called for:

(1) In all institutions at this level where, for various reasons, admissions are selective, steps should be taken to reserve an adequate proportion of the total seats for the economically handicapped students selected on the basis of merit.

(2) All children and youth from economically handicapped families who are admitted should receive free education, in both formal and non-formal streams. They should be given individual attention and guidance (and other relevant facilities) which will enable them to adjust themselves to these institutions and get the largest possible benefit from them.

(3) The talented children from the poor families get a very raw deal in the present system. Many of them go unnoticed because they do not either enter schools or drop out early. They have access mainly

to poor schools which is a great handicap. The culture-loaded selection tests are all against them and they receive little of the personal guidance or tuition they need to overcome their social handicaps. What is even worse, they are often unable to continue their studies because the opportunity costs are very high for them. Well-planned and large-scale efforts are needed to ensure that this talent, which is our precious national asset, is discovered and cultivated. At the elementary stage itself, there must be a sustained nation-wide drive to discover talent and selected children should be enabled to continue their education at the secondary level, through such assistance, including scholarships and placement, as may be necessary in each case. A similar programme should be mounted at the secondary stage as well. The selection tests will have to be specially devised to ensure that the talented children of the poor are not a handicap, and they should be provided with the needed personal guidance and tuition. In fact, it should be an article of faith in the new educational policy that all talented children of the poor families shall be deemed to be the wards of the State and shall be enabled to receive the highest education they desire and are capable of.

We would like to make it clear that we do not propose any reduction in the existing programmes of promoting the education of scheduled castes and tribes. These in fact have to be expanded considerably.

Fees

Secondary and particularly university education are highly subsidised at present because the fees have remained low while the costs have been continually rising. As the subsidy involved in this process goes mostly to the upper and middle classes, they strongly resist the raising of fees. In fact, they exert a continuous pressure for reduction or abolition of fees. There is no justification to continue this inequity; and once free education is assured to the poor, early steps should be taken to increase the fees, in both secondary and university education, and those who can should be required to pay for them in proportion to their ability. This a hard political decision; but there is no escape from it, partly to earn additional resources, partly to keep down pressures on the expansion of full-time institutions, and partly on grounds of social justice. Raising of fees to a realistic level should also make students and parents take a serious view of the frequent closure of schools, colleges, and universities.

The problem of high fee charging and financially independent institutions like public schools or some English medium schools is relevant in this context. It is true that there should be no objection, on financial grounds, to the establishment of private or public educational institutions at the secondary and university stages where the fees charged cover all the costs. But there would be serious objection to them on educational and social grounds because access to such institutions would ordinarily be restricted only to the rich and well-to-do who can afford to pay the high fees charged and thus lead to social segregation.

The best course would, therefore, be to abolish such institutions. But if this is not immediately possible, the minimum essential reform to be adopted, as a transitional measure, is to obligate these institutions to admit at least fifty per cent students, selected on the basis of merit, from the economically and socially handicapped families, and subsidise such students partially to the extent of the cost per child in similar institutions maintained by the government. This may involve a further increase in their fees which are already high. But the step is fully justified on grounds of equity.

Selective Admissions

Should admissions to secondary and university education be selective? The proposal has been stoutly opposed in all quarters and has remained practically unimplemented so far. The principal arguments put forward in its support are three: reduction of educated unemployment; raising of standards; and economy in the use of scarce resources. On the other hand, there are strong pressures for the maintenance of the present policy of open-door access, not only from the upper and middle classes who are the principal beneficiaries of the system, but also from the weaker sections of the society who fear that their chances of vertical mobility through higher education will be considerably reduced if it becomes selective. There is, therefore, no neat and tidy solution to this complex problem and we may have to adopt a pragmatic policy on the following lines:

(1) There should be no selection at the beginning of secondary education (class VIII or IX) because the children are too young.

(2) In all full-time institutions at the post-matriculation stage which receive aid from state funds, proper standards should be maintained and the total number of students to be admitted should be prescribed on the academic basis of facilities available; and selection should be resorted to if the number of applicants exceeds the seats available. In order that this should not adversely affect the interests of the weaker sections, it is necessary to design better and more just methods of selection,

and also to reserve adequate seats for all the underprivileged groups.

(3) All non-formal secondary and higher education should receive encouragement and continue the present policy of open-door access. From this point of view, all public examinations at the secondary and university stages should be open to private candidates who have studied on their own. The facilities for correspondence courses (including library and contact programmes) should also be adequately provided in all the linguistic regions.

These policies will ensure that expansion of facilities in post-elementary education will not be at the cost of quality (which is what often happens at present), that non-formal post-elementary education (which can be self-supporting) shall be available to all who desire it and qualify for it, and that selective admissions, which shall be introduced only in state-supported full-time institutions, will not adversely affect the access of the weaker sections of society to post-matriculation education. The programme will succeed better if there are adequate job opportunities for those who are not selected or who do not propose to go in for further education, if the formal and non-formal channels of education are treated as equal in status for purposes of employment, and if due concession are allowed (i.e., in age of recruitment) to ensure that those who adopt a method of recurrent education (i.e., transferring themselves from school to work and vice-versa according to needs) are at least not at a disadvantage in comparison with those who complete their education at one stretch.

Expansion

As most of the evils in post-elementary education (e.g., dilution of standards, over-expansion, escalation in unit costs and waste of resources) arise from the indiscriminate establishment of new institutions and starting of new courses or increasing the number of students admitted in all sorts of institutions without any regard to academic or economic considerations, perhaps the one major step to regulate the expansion of secondary and higher education is to control the establishment and location of new secondary schools, colleges and universities and the starting of new courses or in increasing the intake in existing institutions. Our policy in this respect should, therefore, be based on the following principles:

(1) The improvement of standards in existing institutions should have priority over starting of new institutions.

(2) No new institutions should be started unless adequate resources are available in terms of men, materials and money.

(3) New secondary schools and colleges should be started only in those backward places where the existing facilities are inadequate or where the need for such institutions is clearly justified. New universities should be established only if their need is established on strong academic grounds.

(4) As pressures for the establishment of these institutions often come from private enterprise, it will be helpful to prescribe rigorous conditions for their recognition or affiliation and to insist on compliance with them.

(5) Every effort has to be made to ensure that all secondary schools and colleges have at least a minimum enrolment which makes them viable and economic. The restraint in establishing new institutions, proper planning of their locations, and the rationalisation, where possible, of the existing

institutions themselves, will assist this programme by increasing enrolments in existing institutions.

(6) No new courses should be started in any institution unless a minimum enrolment is assured. Similarly, the provision of existing courses should be rationalised, wherever possible, and courses which have become outdated or have a low demand should be discontinued. Programmes of sharing of facilities and cooperative teaching will also be of great help in reducing costs and increasing efficiency.

(7) No institution should be allowed to admit students in excess of those for whom reasonable facilities exist.

Before closing this discussion, we must refer to two major problems that have a strong influence on expansion of higher education, viz., (a) the close and long-standing nexus between a degree and a place in the privileged group or a job in the organised sector, especially under government, and (b) the wage-structure we have adopted for educated persons.

(1) The practice of appointing educated persons to jobs under government began more than a hundred and thirty years ago as a method of encouraging people to go in for the new system of education that had been established by the colonial administration. It worked well till about 1921 because the expansion of jobs under government (or in the tertiary sector for which secondary and university education generally prepared their students) could still keep pace with the output of the educational system. But since then, the undesirable consequences of this nexus have come to the fore. To begin with, it over-emphasizes the bread-and-butter objective of secondary and higher education and makes them a

ladder which enables the ambitious to climb into privilege, even as it devalues their academic objective, viz., the production of individuals dedicated to the pursuit of scholarship and excellence. Moreover, the hunt for a place in the privileged sector or a well-paid and secure job in the organised sector creates immense pressures for the expansion of secondary and higher education because they grow more in proportion to the large numbers of aspirants for jobs rather than in relation to the small number of jobs available. This necessarily leads to an over-production of secondary school and college graduates and to large-scale educated unemployment. Instead of dealing with this problem by regulating the output of the educational system, we try to meet the situation by several devious methods such as the appointment of educated persons as teachers within the education system itself, creation of jobs in the organised public sector even in excess of needs (which is really equivalent to disguised under-employment and leads to indiscipline and waste of resources), and upgrading of qualifications required for the posts without any justification or by appointing persons over-qualified for the jobs (which only leads to a devaluation of education). But none of these methods have helped; and what is worse, they have merely increased the pressures for the expansion of higher education still further, sapped the motivation of the students, created unrest and indiscipline on the campuses and lowered the standards even more extensively. A stage has now been reached when a university degree has become almost the minimum educational qualification for any worthwhile job and, at the same time, the distance between a degree and a job has increased so greatly that the process of hunting for a job through higher education has become almost tantamount to a draw in a lottery.

(2) In the same way, the unrealistic and arbitrary wage-structure which we have created and which is far beyond our economic capacity, has led to yet another set of problems and contradictions. On the one hand, it increases the unit cost of education so that further expansion of education becomes more difficult; and on the other hand. it increases the demand for expansion of education by making each job more covetable. Similarly, it decreases the number of jobs we can create by increasing the investment needed per job while it simultaneously increases the number of claimants for the job through an enlarged output of the system. What is even worse, it disturbs the value structure in the academic world itself. An educated person should be an individual who values our tradition of plain living and high thinking and who is close to the people and dedicated to their service. The artificial wage-structure we have evolved for educated persons makes them courtiers rather than seers, increases the distance between them and the people, and converts them from servants into exploiters of the masses. It is, therefore, necessary, not only to break this link between higher education and jobs in the privileged sector, but to transform the present wage-structure itself on egalitarian lines.

If these basic problems have to be tackled satisfactorily, the following are some of the more important measures that can be taken:

(1) The arbitrary, uneconomic and inegalitarian wage-structure should be abandoned, in both the public

and private sectors. A new egalitarian national policy on wages-incomes-prices should be enunciated and enforced in a phased programme spread over not more than ten years.

(2) The qualifications prescribed for jobs in the public sector should be reviewed and the present policy of recruiting over-qualified persons should be abandoned. In fact, it will be found that, for most jobs a pass at the 10+ stage (or 10 + 2 stage) would be enough. Therefore, persons with higher educational qualifications should either be disqualified for these jobs or the age of recruitment to them should be so fixed that graduates would not ordinarily be able to compete. The private sector also could be persuaded to adopt similar policies.

(3) The present system of giving preference to those who have studied in full-time institutions should be abandoned; and in recruitment, persons trained through private study or part-time education should receive at least equal consideration, if not some preference.

(4) Wherever possible, the present practice of selecting persons on the basis of formal education only should be abandoned; and recruitment may be made through special tests which are job-specific and open also to persons who have been trained through non-formal and incidential channels as well. The possession of a degree should not be obligatory for appearing for these tests; and the Union Public Service Commission may give a lead by not requiring a degree for all the competitive examinations it holds, including the IAS and other services.

(5) The tendency to over-professionalise (which in turn over-emphasizes higher education) should be curbed; and work and services should be so organised that more and more tasks are done at the middle or lower levels by paraprofessionals or even nonprofessionals.

Improvement of Standards in Secondary Education

Improvement of standards in secondary education is crucial to the entire educational system because this stage provides the teachers for the elementary schools and students for the colleges and universities. Emphasis should, therefore, be placed on the improvement of standards in secondary education rather than on expansion. This will involve raising the enrolments in every secondary school to an optimum level where it becomes academically viable and economic, a substantial upgrading of facilities in terms of land, buildings and equipment (these are substandard in a large majority of institutions at present), and faculty improvement. This will need a substantial investment of funds, a part of which could be raised from the community.

A thorough reform of the content of secondary education is called for and will be the most significant programme for this purpose. As at the elementary stage, work-experience and social service should become an integral part of secondary education. A diversification and upgrading of the curriculum is necessary on the broad lines recommended by the Education Commission. Unfortunately, several controversies have been raging at present over different aspects of this programme.

(1) The Education Commission recommended that the teaching of science and mathematics should be improved and made compulsory at this stage. This is being objected to on the ground that it affects the

education of girls and the backward classes who are comparatively weak in these subjects. The recommendation is, however, basically sound and inescapable in the modern world. We also do not believe that there is any scientific basis to the argument that girls or backward classes are adversely affected by this recommendation. At the most, they would need some special assistance in the transitional phase. This should be provided.

(2) Some advocate the deepening of the content of secondary education to improve standards and to keep pace with the growing knowledge in the world. Others condemn this effort on the ground that it overloads the children with inert information and tries to convert them into bearers of book-loads or little memory machines. We believe that deepening of content is essential and inescapable. But this can and should be achieved through better methods of teaching and evaluation rather than through a mere overloading of the curriculum as we have been doing so far. Probably some rationalisation and simplification is needed at the lower secondary level. However, at the higher secondary stage, consideration for standards should predominate. Any attempt to reduce the content at this level to bring it within the reach of every aspirant would be fatal. Instead, we should select only those who have the competence to receive education at this level where the first steps towards specialisation are taken.

(3) The problem of nature of content of the lower secondary stage (classes IX-X or VIII-X) has not yet been resolved. The Secondary Education Commission (1952) recommended definite streaming and the Education Commission (1964-66) recommended an undiversified course, but without

a compulsory pass in any subject, the eligibility to further education depending upon the achievement of each student. The latter is definitely a progressive measure and we should gradually move in the direction thus indicated.

(4) Controversies have been raised about the extent to which curricula at the secondary stage should be uniform over all parts of the country. An absolute uniformity is neither possible nor desirable. But it is essential to evolve, through discussion and mutual negotiation between the States, a few broad guidelines regarding (a) avoidence of matters which would impair or harm national integration, and (b) the achievement of broadly comparably standards at the public examinations at the end of class X and class XII which should be regarded as equivalent on a national basis. In this, the Ministry of Education and the NCERT have a significant role to play.

The principal difficulties in resolving the conflicting views is the unrealistic attempt to create a uniform and rigid system in all parts of a vast and plural country like that of ours. As recommended earlier, we should give up this attempt and strive to create a varied, elastic and dynamic system of secondary education which can be best adjusted to local conditions and needs. The idea of creating 'experimental schools' which can, under certain terms and conditions, be allowed to frame their own curricula, should also be adopted and promoted vigorously.

We have been talking of vocationalisation of secondary education for nearly one hundred years; and in spite of all the experiments tried so far, the enrolement in vocational courses at the secondary stage barely exceeds ten per cent of the total. It will be readily agreed that this situation is far from happy and that we should move in a new direction so that the bulk of the students in secondary schools could be prepared to enter the world of work rather than a college or university. This is necessary even in the present situation where only 25 children out of 100 complete the elementary course; and obviously, it will be even more essential when all the 100 children will complete-the elementary course, The basic issues therefore are: who will go in for these vocational courses at the secondary stage and why? What type of vocational courses shall be provided at the secondary stage and how? It is to these difficult problems that we have not been able to find satisfactory solutions.

Let us begin at the end of the elementary stage and ask ourselves: who will go in for secondary education when everyone completes elementary education and the age of marriage is raised to 18 for girls and 21 for boys? Some may think that the studies at the secondary level are too difficult and may decide to step off. Others may find the opportunity costs of secondary education to be too high and may decide to leave. This situation should be accepted with one reservation, viz., talented children who cannot proceed further due to economic reasons should be assisted to continue their education. Even among those who decide to continue their studies, some may decide not to enter upon a regular secondary course, but to take vocational courses of various durations and to prepare themselves for specific careers. There should, therefore, be adequate provision for such courses which form the first stage of vocationalisation. This aspect has not received adequate attention so far and needs emphasis in the years ahead.

A more serious attempt at vocational education will have to be made at higher secondary stage where a much larger proportion of students may decide to go in, not for the university preparatory courses, but for the vocational courses which would prepare them for various kinds of employment opportunities, including self-employment. There are already a number of courses which begin at this level and prepare for various jobs in the organised sector (polytechnics, most courses in ITI, teacher-training programmes, agricultural or forestry schools, correspondence, type-writing, shorthand, and other secretarial courses, etc.). But obviously the scope of these could be enlarged, especially if we include programmes of self-employment or entrepreneurship, in various fields such as health, agriculture, industry, or management. Considerable work is needed for the designing of these courses on the basis of careful studies of local situations regarding employment opportunities available in the immediate future.

The vocational courses may be terminal in the sense that students will step off the educational ladder at these points and enter the world of work. But there should be adequate opportunity and provision for these students to rejoin the educational stream, if and when necessary, and to get vertical mobility. The lack of popularity of these courses at present is also another problem to faced. But let it be emphasized that the extent to which students will opt for these courses will depend upon the development of the economy, the choice of technology the availability of jobs, the narrowing down of the wage-structure between different levels of workers and especially as between the blue and white collar categories, the extent to which we can assure these students opportunities for further education and vertical mobility, the extent to which admissions to the academic course preparatory to the university become selective, and the discontinuance of the present practice of recruiting highly educated persons for middle-level jobs. What is said here will also apply to some vocational courses of a higher type which can be provided after the higher secondary stage. These will form the third level of vocational courses.

At present, most of our vocational courses are school-based and a large proportion of students who join them do so on an experimental basis before they have definitely decided upon a career or have been selected for a specific job. We should like to emphasize that this process, while essential in some cases, is wasteful and less efficient. Wherever possible, we should try to provide post-decision or post-selection vocational courses. In all such cases, there is good motivation and an optimum utilisation of available scarce resources. Secondly, there should be a considerable increase in industry-based vocational courses so that vocations are 'educationalised' instead of vocationalising education. Such a programme may even be made obligatory on industries and certain grant-in-aid made available to them for the purpose if necessary. Thirdly, there should be an adequate provision for sandwich courses and for regular apprenticeship training.

Higher Education and Research

Higher education in India presents a saga of a few achievements and many failures. Its main contribution is that it has helped to create a large stock of high level trained manpower (some of which is extremely competent) and to build a good indigenous capability in research. We have also some creditable achievements in science and technology and in agricultural, engineering, and medical education which has helped us to develop a modern industrial sector, to promote agricultural development through the introduction of modern technology, and to build up a network of high quality modern health services. We have also been able to expand the university base and to establish some centres of advanced study in the universities as well as a few high quality institutions of teaching and research outside the university system. But its failures are even greater.

The vast bulk of the institutions, mostly affiliated colleges of general education, maintain poor standards and many of them are too small to be academically viable or financially economic. The enrolments have increased inordinately; and, as the economy has not grown in proportion, higher education converts, on a large scale, the uneducated underemployment or unemployment (which is mute, unorganised, and without a nuisance value) into educated'. urban unemployment.

As stated earlier, this also saps student motivation, creates unrest on the campus, and leads to further deterioration of standards. The courses provided are often irrelevant and undemanding and not sufficiently modernised and diversified; the method of teaching over-emphasize lectures and the examinations continue to be external and traditional. The teaching and learning materials leave a good deal to be desired and the continued use of English as medium of instruction creates difficult problems in teaching, learning or communication and lowers the standards still further, besides creating a wall between the intelligentsia and the people.

Perhaps the worst aspect of the problem is the continuous crisis situation in higher education. Over the past fifteen years or so, the university system in India is passing from crisis to crisis arising out of rapid and unplanned expansion, inadequate finances, lowering of standards, agitations by teachers. students and karamcharis which paralyse university life, official and political interference, and weakness of administration (bordering virtually on collapse in some areas) which fails to rise up to the challenges of the situation and is too paralysed to act on sound academic principles by the atmosphere of violence created on the campus by political vested interests, an ill-disciplined minority among students and anti-social elements.

The emergency created a temporary peace in this situation. But that can hardly be called a solution and a tremendous price had to be paid for it in terms of the loss of academic freedom. With the withdrawal of emergency, all the old familiar scenes of unrest, violence, and crisis are again being re-enacted on the campus, especially as the basic causes of the situation still continue to operate. Very naturally people feel more concerned about the dysfunctioning of higher education than of any other stage of our educational system; and this is, therefore, the one area in which determined action is called for on a priority basis. Desperate situations call for desperate remedies; and some heroic measures are often suggested to improve the situation.

(1) The first is the recommendation of the C.D. Deshmukh Committee that a compulsory national service of one year should be obligatory on a student, who has completed the secondary school, before he is admitted to the college. This is a good programme on its own merits. But its contribution to the resolution of the present crisis situation in higher education is at best doubtful. The programme also involves a very high financial investment which we may not be able to afford and requires an immense organisational effort which we may not be able to mount up. On the other hand, both the financial and organisational issues will become much easier if' the national service programme is integrated with the undergraduate course.

(2) The second is the proposal that all colleges and universities should be closed for a year and the students and teachers involved in programmes of national and social service in general and in transforming the educational system in particular. The organisational implications of this programme

are even more formidable than those of the Deshmukh proposal. It may also be emphasized that the plan will be effective only if it is well implemented and if we are in a position to utilise the services of teachers and students in meaningful and challenging programmes; and it will be equally unproductive or even counter-productive if this cannot be done.

All things considered, one sees no short-cuts to a radical transformation of the system which will have to be attempted through a well-planned, sustained and vigorous programme in spite of all the difficulties involved. It was pointed out earlier that the organisation of a mass movement is absolutely essential if programmes of adult and elementary education have to succeed. In secondary and higher education, the position is different: no significant improvement is possible at these stages unless some hard decisions are taken, both by politicians and academics.

(1) Some of the hard political decisions to be made will include,

- — regulation of the over-all expansion of higher education, the introduction of the system of double pricing under which the poor will get free education and others will have to pay higher fees according to their ability, and reduction of subsidies, both direct and indirect, which go to the rich and well to-do side by side with an increase in those which go the poor;
- — introduction of selective admissions with the necessary safeguards for the weaker sections;
- — adoption of measures which will eventually delink jobs from degrees;
- — maintenance of discipline; and

— protection of university autonomy and full political support without political interference.

(2) The implementation of a national language policy. This is an example of a decision which is both political and academic and where politicians and academics will have to collaborate meaningfully.

(3) There are also several decisions which the academic community itself is responsible to make and implement. These include,

— exercise of academic freedom with courage to function as a critic of society;

— earning and continually deserving autonomy through the rectitude and quality of administration, level of academic performance and the extent of services to the local community and the nation;

— sharing and passing down the autonomy from the universities to their departments and affiliated colleges which, in turn, should share it with teachers and students;

— involving students intimately in the entire life of the university; and

— making radical changes in the content of education and in the methods of teaching and evaluation.

It is unfortunate that -most of the decisions in these matters are not being made, and the different groups seem to be acting at cross-purposes with one another. No solution of the complex and difficult problems facing secondary and university education can come this way. Progress will be possible only if all the agencies involved -the Centre, the State, the teachers, the students, and the public at large -play their assigned roles with a sense of commitment and responsibility.

Bibliography

Ahmad, A. and S.C. Nuna, "Inequity in the Literacy Levels of Population in Maharashtra", in Moonis Raza (ed.), *Educational Planning - A Long Term Perspectives,* New Delhi, NIEPA, 1985.

_____________ , "Tribal Education: Shadows of an Uncertain Future", *Journal of Educational Planning and Administration,* Special Issue on Equity in Education, Vol. 1, No. 2, pp. 96-107, 1987.

Carron, Gabriel and Chau Ta Ngoc (eds.), "Regional Disparities in Educational Development: Diagnosis and Policies for Reduction", Paris: IIEP, 1980..

Gosal, G.S., "Literacy in India - An Interpretive Study", *Rural Sociology,* 29. No. 3, September, pp. 261-77, 1964.

_____________ ., "Regional Aspects of Rural Literacy in India", Presidential Address, Transactions of the Indian Council of Geographers, 1967.

Government of India, *The Report of the University Education Commission,* Vol. 1, New Delhi : Ministry of Education, 1970.

Jencks, Christopher, *Inequality,* New York : Basic Books, 1972..

Krishan, Gopal and Madhav Shyam, "Spatial Perspective on Progress of Female Literacy in India: 1901-1971", *Pacific Viewpoint,* 14, pp. 203-6, 1973.

Krishan, Gopal and Madhav Shyam, "Pattern of City Literacy", *Economic and Political Weekly,* 9, No. 20, May 18, 1974.

Madan, T.N., "Education of Tribal India", *The Eastern Anthropologist,* Vol. V. (4) pp. 179-82, 1951.

NCERT, "Education and National Development", *Report of the Education Commission,* 1964-66, New Delhi, 1971.

Nuna, S.C., "Educational Statistics in India: A Need for Appraisal", *Progressive Educational Herald,* Vol. 1, No. 2, pp. 82-86, 1987.

_____________ ., *Education and Development,* NIEPA, New Delhi, **1987.**

Nurullah, S. and J.P. Naik, "A Students History of Education in India, New Delhi: Macmillan & Co., 1974.

Premi, M. K., "Educational Planning in India", New Delhi : Sterling, 1972.

Raza. Moonis, A. Ahmad and S.C. Nuna, "Tribal Literacy in India: The Relional Dimension", *Occasional Paper 9*, NIEPA, New Delhi, 1985.

Ruhela, S.P., "Social Determinants of Educability in India," *Papers in the Sociological Context of Indian Education*, New Delhi: Jain Brothers, 1969.

Sopher, David E., "A Measure of Disparity", *Professional Geographer*, 26, pp. 389-92, 1974.

Subba Rao, B., *Personality of India*, Baroda, M.S. University, 1958.

Index